CW00497014

Should I Flush My Goldfish Down The Loo?

Should I Flush My Goldfish Down The Loo?

and other
Modern Morals

Joe Joseph

HODDER &
STOUGHTON

First published in Great Britain in 2007

1

British Library Cataloguing in Publication Data
A record for this book is available from the British Library

ISBN 978 0340 954683

Typeset in New Caledonia and Bokka by
Avon DataSet Ltd,
Bidford on Avon, Warwickshire

Printed and bound in Great Britain by
Clays Ltd, St Ives plc

The paper and board used in this paperback are natural recyclable products made from wood grown in sustainable forests. The manufacturing processes conform to the environmental regulations of the country of origin.

Hodder & Stoughton
A Division of Hodder Headline Ltd
338 Euston Road
London NW1 3BH
www.madaboutbooks.com

For Jane, Thomas, Charles and Eliza

CONTENTS

Acknowledgements

For their decision to invite me to take on the role of *The Times*'s ethical arbiter as author of a new, daily 'Modern Morals' column – without ever making it sound like they might be playing some kind of a practical joke – I owe a huge debt to the editor of *The Times*, Robert Thomson, and to Sandra Parsons, editor of *Times 2*, whose support, advice and encouragement have been invaluable.

My thanks also to Ben Preston, Anne Spackman and David Chappell at *The Times*, and to Dominic Young and James Heath of News International, who in various ways all helped to launch and smooth the progress of the column, or else played midwife to its rebirth here in a tweaked and modified form.

Between them, all these colleagues have helped me to discover moral principles I never knew I had; and mostly cannot afford.

The subeditors on *Times 2* – unsung heroes of any newspaper – have rescued me from many embarrassments by spotting and correcting errors. The grammatical ones, at any rate. Lamentable errors of judgement remain all my own.

Without Judith Longman's enthusiasm at Hodder, this book might not have taxied to the runway. Robert Kirby and Katie Bayer at PFD were invaluable in ensuring that it then took off smoothly.

I am deeply indebted, of course, to readers of *The Times*,

who have bombarded me with a ceaseless supply of ethical dilemmas to explore. Which leads me to my final volley of thanks – which is addressed to moral transgressors everywhere . . . without whom this book would not have been possible.

INTRODUCTION

'There is always a right way and a wrong way, and the wrong way always seems the more reasonable'

George Moore

Mark Twain once sent a telegram to a dozen friends saying, 'FLEE AT ONCE – ALL IS DISCOVERED', and they all left town immediately. And the moral of this story? The moral is that nobody sends telegrams any more and Mark Twain would today have had to text them instead. He would have had to write: 'Fl once. All Dscvrd', to which his startled and anxious friends would immediately have responded by saying: '*WHAT?* Mark . . . have you been smoking something again?'

No, hang on! The actual moral of this story is that everyone has a guilty secret. None of us is as white as snow; or even as white as Michael Jackson's complexion. It shows that not only do we all do things that we shouldn't, but also that we generally have a pretty shrewd idea of when, where and how we shouldn't have done them (except, maybe, OJ Simpson).

That makes morals seem worthy and just a little cheerless, doesn't it, like eating bread that's so full of nutritious wholegrain fibre that you need a chainsaw to cut it?

This probably explains why the ethics world (wouldn't that make a fascinating theme park? 'Visit *Ethicsworld* and go to Hell in a handcart! . . . Car parking available for visitors who have no moral qualms about carbon emissions . . . Patrons must all keep to the right path') likes to put enough meat on any argument for everyone to be able to have a good chew, whatever their viewpoint. The understanding is that there are two ways of looking at any issue; though not necessarily that one way is superior to the other (EXAMPLE: 'Just because there are some people who passionately believe that Sylvester Stallone is painfully talentless, that doesn't mean there aren't plenty of others who believe he should be maimed to prevent him making any more movies').

It's ethics as Escher drawing, if you like: look at a moral problem this way and one image swims into view; cock your head and squint at it from another direction and you glimpse a very different picture. (This, of course, implies that ethicists actually themselves behave in the way they suggest to us that we all should, rather than merely making moral pronounce-ments which make them sound virtuous; and frankly you can't help feeling, when you look at some of the self-proclaimed moralists who've been doing the telling over the centuries, that this seems about as likely as Lindsay Lohan remembering to wear underwear in public two days running. Samuel Johnson certainly counted himself among the sceptics: 'Be not too hasty to admire the teachers of morality,' he hissed. 'They discourse like angels, but they live like men.')

Yet far from being a criticism, you might wonder if this room for manoeuvre, this convenient gap between words and deeds, isn't what gives ethics some of its appeal. Because there are always people within useful tut-tutting distance of us who appear to be living *a lot* more 'like men' than we are, aren't there? Somehow we never seem to find it very hard – however low we ourselves might stoop, morality-wise – to identify plenty of others all around us who are behaving even more immorally than us.

So how do such people distinguish themselves to us? Generally speaking, they are people who might seem, on the surface, to be behaving just as badly as we are – but with the crucial difference that *they appear to be having a lot more fun while they're doing so*. This enjoyment is what makes their behaviour that bit more shameless.

This, basically, is the position of the Stoics (who are not the sort of people you want to be putting at the top of your party invitation list). It works roughly like this: the more fun something is, the higher the chances of its being regarded as immoral (think of it in terms of food: have you noticed that the better a dish tastes, the more likely it is that each mouthful contains enough calories to sustain the population of Alaska through an entire winter? It's a bit like that. On the other hand, adhering to a virtuous life of monastic self-denial is the equivalent of subsisting on steamed tofu). In every group of people there is always one person who is behaving more immorally than everyone else. If you can't work out which person in your circle is the one behaving more immorally than everyone else, then the chances are that the person is you.

Now, it might strike you that there is not all that much room for ethical debate in modern life, because no two sane, rational people would hold wildly diverging views on most moral issues: we all tend to share an instinctive sense of the difference between right and wrong, don't we? For instance, most people would find the idea of, say, sleeping with their daughter, or with a sibling, repugnant; or the notion of killing your wife to get your hands on her money to be wholly immoral. Even Donald Trump realised he'd crossed an invisible line when, in a loose-tongued moment, he said that his daughter was so attractive that if she weren't his daughter he might be dating her.

But not all moral dilemmas are so easily resolved. Take the

invasion of Iraq: was that morally right, even if Saddam proved not to be harbouring weapons of mass destruction, because he was a murderous dictator who tyrannised his people? Yes? Or euthanasia: are you all for it? What about testing potentially life-saving medicines on rabbits? Spending £100 to cure a sick child in London, rather than spending that same £100 to cure 100 sick children in Africa: is that selfish, or sensible? Torturing a prisoner of war, if such torture will reveal the whereabouts of a ruthless warmonger who would go on to kill thousands more innocent people if not stopped? Hmmm . . . never justifiable? Or could it sometimes be worth holding your nose and doing it?

What about if the lives of five patients needing different organ transplants could be saved if a surgeon harvested the necessary organs from a healthy young man who has just walked in to the hospital to donate blood (to pick a hypothetical example used recently by Harvard researchers to gauge the public's ethical temperature)? Wouldn't it be worth rescuing five lives for the loss of just one? Most of us would think not; that saving the five patients would not justify the murder of an innocent man.

But wait a second! What if the young man happened to be a known serial killer? Or a particularly repellent character from a TV reality show? (JUDGE: 'Does the defendant wish to alert the court to any mitigating circumstances which might explain what provoked him to commit this terrible murder?' DEFENDANT'S BARRISTER: 'Your Honour, the victim was a migraine-inducing housemate on *Celebrity Big Brother.*' JUDGE: 'Why the hell didn't you mention this earlier? Case dismissed').

Yet not all ethical dilemmas on which society routinely has to adjudicate are so straightforward to answer as the organ-donor example: a hospital with limited funds for operations might have to decide, say, whether a child with many years still to live should take precedence over an octogenarian. Should a political party jettison some of its principles, if doing so would enable it to win an election and thus to enact laws it believes will benefit the country – or stay uncompromised, but in Opposition?

Ernest Hemingway, with trademark economy, said: 'I know only that what is moral is what you feel good after and what is immoral is what you feel bad after' (Hemingway was evidently not a Stoic). But even this feel-good litmus test can give blurry results: if he felt good after watching a bullfight, would that make bullfighting morally OK?

When people say that ethics and morality are about doing the right thing in the right situation they don't mean proclaiming: 'Me? Watch Jade Goody on TV? Are you mad? I'd rather shuck oysters with my bare teeth!' When philosophers say that ethics is about how we ought to live, they don't mean it the same way the editor of an architectural style magazine, or a foie-gras-loving chef, might mean it. And anyway, behaving correctly, or doing good, may count for less than just discouraging people from doing bad. As the economist Milton Friedman saw it, the challenge is how to construct a world in which immoral people can do the least harm, 'not how to enable moral people to do the most good'. Because when you come right down to it, nobody likes a smug moral do-gooder. H.L. Mencken's objection to Puritans was 'not that they try to make us think as they do, but that they try to make us do as they think'.

So what, then, if we just go through life minding our own business, not preaching prissily to others, not doing anyone else any harm, breaking no laws, and generally keeping ourselves out of harm's way? Is that an ethically noble prescription for life?

Maybe not. Dante reckoned that 'the hottest places in Hell are reserved for those who, in a time of great moral crisis, maintain their neutrality'. Who knows? It's possible that the scriptwriters of *Seinfeld* thought along the same lines as Dante, because in the finale of the US sitcom, the show's stars – a quartet of famously self-absorbed New Yorkers – are prosecuted for having failed to come to the aid of a mugging victim. The foursome are found guilty and jailed under a newly enacted 'Good Samaritan' law, after the court's judge brushes aside their lawyer's protest that there is 'no such thing as a guilty bystander'. Is there?

It's easy enough to see morality and ethics as subjects like Greek and quantum theory – subjects which people study in universities, but which have as much relevance to your everyday life as the price of toothbrushes in Tonga. But the *Seinfeld* finale can remind us that it's important to have some moral principles to guide you through life. If these fail you, then find better ones. If you fail them, why not keep a few more malleable spares in reserve? If nothing else, you'll feel good for having done so. And that's a moral virtue in itself. Ernest Hemingway said so, didn't he?

This book brings together many of the moral dilemmas of everyday life – encountered at home; abroad; some at work; with friends; or with family; often with strangers – sent to me by readers of *The Times*, and my attempts to offer answers that seemed to me morally plausible, without being overly solemn. Mostly not solemn at all, in fact.

It turns out that what keeps people up at night is not so much whether God exists and whether his Ten Commandments should be obeyed, but whether you should feel guilty about not alerting a rude shopkeeper who has handed you too much change; or whether it's unethical to tell white lies for a friend's job reference; or wrong to refuse to help your son with exam coursework projects, when other parents are helping their children to attain top grades; or knowingly to pass on a forged £20 note that some cad has palmed off on you; or if it's immoral for a man to spend £275 on a shirt for himself; or for you to sell your university essays to lazier fellow students; or whether you have any right – or even a duty – to tell a friend who is so grossly overweight that their clothes now all carry Size XXXXL labels, as if they're name-tags on sweaters belonging to a Roman emperor, that maybe their appetite is out of control.

If, after reading this book, you're still struggling to steer a course through these challenging waters, and to work out what to do for the best in the face of a vexing ethical dilemma that crops up in your daily life, Mencken minted a convenient guide: 'Morality is the theory that every human act must either be right or wrong and that 99 per cent of them are wrong.' Does that make everything simpler for you?

I Love Affairs

*'My own belief is that there is
hardly anyone whose sexual life,
if it were broadcast, would not
fill the world at large with
surprise and horror'*

W. Somerset Maugham

Fish has its chips

I returned home to discover that one of my goldfish was very unwell. I extracted it from the bowl, to prevent it infecting the rest, and put it into isolation in a water-filled jar, hoping that it might recover. But when my partner came home, he just wanted to flush the poorly goldfish down the lavatory. Having discovered that our views on the sanctity of life are so far apart, should I leave him?

That sort of depends on whether you yourself fit conveniently down the lavatory. That might then give you some inkling whether – should your partner arrive home one night to find you looking a little poorly – he might idly dispatch you, too, by the same method that he's now recommending for your sick goldfish.

I would suggest taking your pet to a vet; but you wonder whether they even bother to teach a 'goldfish module' in veterinary degrees. Where's the money in it? I mean, who pays to have their pet goldfish undergo gill-replacement surgery? To a vet, fiddling around with something as tiny as a goldfish is like bothering with prising open those securely sealed pistachio nuts: life's just too short.

But although a lowly goldfish might seem like small fry in the giant Darwinian pattern of life, you do wonder whether the sickly condition of your fish doesn't perhaps cast a sceptical light on those health practitioners who say the brain is so powerful that it can overcome all illnesses in your body; you know, mind over matter, and all that. I mean, a goldfish famously has a memory span so short it can barely even remember it's a goldfish. That would suggest your goldfish shouldn't be able to remember from one minute to the next that it even is sick. Thus its mind should not be able constantly to relay reinforcing 'You are ill' messages to its body. That tells you something, doesn't it? Though maybe not enough to fill a whole vet-school module.

Varsity match

I recently visited a female friend from earlier university days whom I've known for many years. After a drunken party we ended up sleeping in bed together all night. Should I feel guilty about this, given that nothing occurred between us, but that I have a wife who wouldn't be too thrilled to find out that I'd shared a bed with another woman?

Feeling guilty is not the same as being guilty. Then again, if you feel guilty, even when you're not guilty, it's possible you sense you've been enjoying yourself just a little more than maybe you should have been.

Alternatively, feeling guilty when you're not guilty is a sign that you've not been enjoying yourself anywhere near as much as people examining the evidence will imagine you will have been; which is about as maddening and unfair as any fix can get.

When a jury has to choose whether someone is guilty or innocent, it weighs up the evidence and decides which sounds more plausible: the case for the prosecution, or that for the defence. It's essentially a hunch, embroidered by fragments of evidence; like *Cluedo* for grown-ups. In your circumstances, many jurors might well veer towards a hunch of guilty. But jurors also have a halfway house. If they haven't been convinced either way, they can acquit, which is legalese for 'Hmmm. Not sure'. But 'acquit' is not an option that exists in real life. No squabble between a man and wife ever ended with one of them agreeing to acquit the other. If you report to your wife what happened, she might well imagine you to be guilty. But if you don't report your bed-sharing experience, and she finds out and realises that you hid it from her, she'll find you 'guilty as hell', a verdict unknown in real courtrooms on account of its being so ferocious that no judge has ever had the stomach to impose it.

Screen play

? *My partner has grown obsessed with internet pornography. After I found out about it, he promised he would stop. But he hasn't. As soon as I leave the house, he logs on. When he works from home, he logs on. If I go out in the evenings, he logs on. I'm not a prude in the bedroom, so I don't understand why he has to do this. Am I wrong to be so upset by his deceit?*

Now you mention it, there does seem to be an eerie correlation between the rise in the number of people working at home and the growth of internet pornography. It is also true that pornography seems to be a market targeted more at men than women; possibly because women are often confused by porn films, on account of their straining to locate an actual plot.

Women also find it implausible that there are so many women so luxuriantly buxom that their breasts experience different weather from the rest of their body; or who can have sex so many times a day with visiting tradesmen, while never once removing their stilettos. But this is to misunderstand pornography: it's like damning a *James Bond* movie for not painting a realistic picture of how MI6 agents go about keeping the nation safe from madmen seeking world domination. Nor can women understand some men's fascination with watching two women in bed together (I'll explain: men watch only to pick up tips on how to make love to a woman properly).

What is it you find immoral: watching pornography, or that your partner lies about doing so? Some people find all pornography immoral – the only trouble being that the line where erotica trips over into porn varies with tastes and the times. Providing that the sites your partner visits are not the sort they can arrest you for, many might regard the lying as more unethical than the porn-watching.

Truly, madly, deeply

I think I am in love with my boyfriend. We have been together for five months. Do I have a moral obligation to tell him that I love him?

A moral obligation? It's certainly reassuring for a man to hear that his girlfriend loves him, because many men feel that such a commitment leads the relationship into a new phase of openness and honesty; a phase where the man can spend an evening at home with his girl, watching a movie, sipping red wine and, instead of having to get up every half hour, can break wind straight into the sofa cushion, just as he does when he's alone.

If you expect the man to reciprocate, though, you may be waiting a long time. It's not that he doesn't feel the same way about you; or that he regards the word 'love' as meaningless. It's because men know how much weight women attach to it that men do not like to use the word loosely.

It's like this. Say you go out to dinner. A woman looks at the menu, spots linguine with clams and says: 'I love linguine with clams! I've chosen.' It's a decision made. A decision she's happy with. She might find another dish on the menu that would give her equal pleasure – but not necessarily more pleasure.

Now, a man might also like linguine. But he knows he also likes steak. With chips. And turbot. He likes to be sure that he's made the right choice. A man can be handed a menu that's longer than Al Gore's face after the Florida hanging-chad recount and he'll still ask the waiter whether there are any specials on the menu tonight: he wouldn't want to think that he'd committed himself without exploring all the options.

So you may feel a moral obligation to yourself to declare your love. Just don't expect your boyfriend to respond immediately. Unless you're offering chips on the side.

Festive joy

I had a fling at a music festival with a woman who, I later learnt, had graduated from university last year and was in work. I told her that I was at Manchester University, without mentioning that I was starting only this September, knowing that she would presume I was older

than my actual age of eighteen. I never directly lied to her.
But I never told her the full truth, either. Should I have
done?

Well, it hardly sounds as if the two of you are Benjamin
Braddock and Mrs Robinson, but it's true that even small age
gaps can seem significant when you're still relatively young.

When you're ten, for instance, a twenty-year-old seems a
very distant fellow. But by the time you reach the age of sixty,
and that twenty-year-old is now seventy, the age gap has
shrivelled through some strange mathematical trick that
Einstein probably explained through his Theory of Relativity.
But it doesn't matter, because it's at around that stage in their
lives that people start camouflaging their true age, anyway –
some through plastic surgery; others by translating their age
into dog years (*'If I were a labrador, I'd be ten!'*), and then
further bamboozling people by converting the dog years into
something else (*'That's two hectares in metric, you know!'*).

You didn't go out of your way to tell her how old you are,
and she didn't go out of her way to find out. Possibly she didn't
care; possibly she had livelier plans on her mind than
comparing birth certificates. What with gap years and mature
students, the ages of students even in the same year at
university can vary widely. As long as she wasn't just using you
to test the efficiency of her new denture fixative, chances are
the age gap wasn't too serious.

Femme fatale

? *A foreign friend has a knack for wrapping men*
around her little finger. While staying with me at
university she became attracted to another friend who,

though seemingly a decent chap, is wont to take advantage.
Each has since asked me for the other's contact details. Am
I morally bound to play Cupid, or should I refuse to
matchmake a couple when it will probably end in tears?

How dull would the world be if a sober judging panel adjudicated on the likely suitability of each pairing every time a man and woman took a shine to one another!

Where would we turn to for amusement if Britney Spears did not occasionally get married for twenty-four hours in Las Vegas; or if Donald Trump didn't keep trading in his blondes for newer models, as if they were old Chevys showing a bit of rust around the wheel arches; or if Elizabeth Taylor hadn't married so many times that she ran out of new men to wed, and had to start marrying the same husband all over again? Joan Collins weds men so young that you wonder if she first flips a coin to decide whether to marry them or adopt them.

Mickey Rooney's marriage has lasted more than twenty years. But he had seven previous failed marriages, during which time the idea of seeking his advice on how to stay married would have seemed as laughable as seeking John Major's advice on how to electrify an audience.

So, you don't have a moral obligation to matchmake. But nor do you have a moral duty to keep apart two people who are old enough to make their own mistakes. When Harpo Marx asked Robert Benchley, of *The New Yorker*, what he thought of his fiancée, the writer said: 'She's a lovely girl. She deserves a good husband. Marry her before she finds one.' Now, *that's* what you call a friend.

In-the-club class

? *Newlyweds who were heading to America on honeymoon arrived at Heathrow during the recent terrorist scare only to join a long queue. Airline officials, misinterpreting the significance of the woman's loose-fitting frock, sped the couple through check-in by upgrading them to Club Class. She was not pregnant. How wrong was she to stay silent?*

And who still dares to say that the Devil does not find new ways to tempt us?

A lot of the blame in this case clearly falls on the airline officials, who made the mistake of making assumptions about a woman's pregnant state without first waiting to be told. You ask a woman only once when her baby is due – to receive the curt reply (a) I'm not pregnant, or (b) I gave birth a month ago – to know that you must never, ever ask this question again. Once you've made that error, you could then spot a woman as slim as spaghetti, preceded by a tummy that made her look as if she'd just swallowed a medicine ball without chewing it first, and you would just ignore the bump until she mentioned it first.

The only time you can safely be first to raise the subject is if you were in the delivery room, and thus had first-hand proof that she'd given birth; or if she is one of these modern mothers who wears a piece of the placenta around her neck on a chain as jewellery.

But the airline officials meant well. The woman behaved shamefully; not only by mocking their show of consideration but, more importantly, by depriving a genuinely needy passenger from being spared distress. It would have served her right if she had been refused Club Class quantities of alcohol during the flight, on the assumption that she obviously wouldn't be drinking while pregnant.

Parting gifts

> *After being with a lady for a year and a half, during which time I gave her many thousands of pounds' worth of gifts, financial help, furniture for her house and help for her son, I was dumped. Her parting comment was that she didn't like me, and had never liked me. The dumping I can accept. But, morally, have I any claim to items that I gave her quite freely?*

You're in danger of sounding like the man who can always remember each occasion he has had sex because he keeps all the receipts. It's a sad fact of life that while there are women who hitch up with men for nothing but love, even though their partners happen to be as rich as a Rockefeller – Anna Nicole Smith, to pick one example – there are others who are a little more mercenary.

Spending money willingly on a woman while you're sharing your lives might feel like adding enough to the pot in a hand of poker to keep yourself in the game: you're interested, generous, committed up to a point, but still keeping most of your chips close to you until such time as you think to yourself: 'You know, this isn't too bad a hand I've got here. It may even be the best hand I'll get. So I'm going to go all in.'

And it's only when you shove all your chips on to the table that you see what cards the other player has been concealing. Sometimes you strike it lucky; at other times your confidence proves misplaced. But when you lose in poker, you can't ask for your chips back. In life it's the same. If you had qualms about opening your wallet, you needed to have registered them at the time. To call in the cash now would be like inviting friends to stay for the weekend and then, because you'd all fallen out by Sunday night over an argument, billing them for board and lodging.

Breakfast Serial

A young gay man working in a shop where I buy my breakfast on weekday mornings undercharges me and/or gives me free breakfast items. I used to find this amusing, but now feel awkward. I don't want him to get into trouble, but nor do I feel it right that the shop's owner is being short-changed. I am also concerned about what the young man in the shop expects in return.

When you say you are beginning to worry about what the gay man in the shop might be expecting to happen next in this drama, I'm assuming you're not so much worried that he might be thinking of breaking into your house at night and rearranging the furniture and plumping up the cushions. Would that be fair? Let's also assume that his regularly undercharging you is not down to a numeracy problem.

So now what? The man behind the counter has behaved unethically by wining and dining you – breakfasting you, at any rate – at the shop owner's expense rather than at his own. But what about you? If the server were a woman you considered a cutie, would you still feel uncomfortable at this prolonged, teasing seduction by croissant and cappuccino? You wouldn't? What's that you say, you might actually encourage her? Then can you understand why the man behind the coffee counter might feel confused by your sudden *froideur* and anxiety?

I doubt he has plans to foist himself on you, though he might be forgiven for assuming that since his small coded gestures didn't meet a businesslike response of, 'I think my bill comes to £4.50, not £2.50', or, 'Actually, I didn't order this blueberry muffin', you were sending him coded messages back.

You could always have bought your breakfast elsewhere. But you evidently like to eat your cake and have it.

Mail Sex

? *I suspect that my boyfriend's 'platonic' internet pen pal has become his lover. He says that they are nothing more than friends, and that there's no sexual intimacy between them. I am certain that he is lying. I do not want to invade his privacy, but neither do I want to live with the uncertainty and the stress. Should I hack into his e-mails to find out whether he is cheating?*

You want to satisfy your curiosity? Then go ahead and hack into your boyfriend's e-mail account (although beware reading too much into what you find there: the avalanche of e-mails he has in his inbox offering to make him the size of King Kong doesn't mean that your boyfriend is in daily negotiation with Florida-based surgeons specialising in penis enlargements that would make even Errol Flynn's eyes water. Nor is it likely that he is racking up hefty bills for prescription drugs; or seeking insider stock-market tips about companies that have a financial shelf life shorter than that of milk; or that he cares what Sally wrote, or what John wrote).

If, on the other hand, you wish to behave ethically, then, no, you should not hack into your man's e-mails. It is not just that it's a tawdry thing to do to someone you wish to trust; or even that it's a tawdry thing to do to yourself; it's that you cannot win either way.

What if you were to discover that your boyfriend is, indeed, canoodling in cyberspace with his pen pal? Then your relationship is shattered. If you find out that he was telling the truth, and is not flirting on the net, your relationship is also shot, because it will now be your boyfriend who'll be wary of trusting you. Jealousy is like peering through a telescope while on mescalin: you see many things more clearly; but you also see a lot of things that aren't there.

No, worst man

? *I asked an old friend to be my best man. But since happily accepting, this friend seems to have lost interest in the duties and responsibilities associated with the wedding. It is clear to me that I chose the wrong person, and I should like to replace him with a better candidate. Would it be wrong to relieve my useless so-called friend of his duties?*

You'd think that by the time you got to choosing a best man you would know which friend you could trust to fulfil the traditional best-man duties of looking after the ring; making a speech; calming the groom's anxiety about long-term commitment by assuring him that 'Till death us do part' has now been superseded by 'Until my swami tells me you're cramping my chakras'; and drafting a plausible alibi for his fiancée, Susie, as to how the groom-to-be ended his stag night wearing a satin thong, stinking of Chanel, and with a nipple ring around his front tooth, the other end of the ring being still secured to the nipple of the transvestite cabaret artiste to whom it belonged (*'Susie, we were approached by these women who were moaning about how their thongs were chafing and wondered if we'd swap underwear just for the evening to help them out, when one of them accidentally spilt a scent bottle all over us, and the odour made your future husband reel into the bosom of a cabaret dancer who happened to be on her – only it turned out to be on his – way to that night's performance. Isn't life so weird sometimes, Susie?'*).

Having chosen poorly, you cannot now sack your friend as best man. Chances are that your fiancée will, in any case, make sure that all runs smoothly. Nobody relies on the groom or the best man to do anything at a wedding apart from turn up: even if not in their own underwear.

Mind the gap

? *A friend's daughter is seeing a much older man with a dubious history. Her family are unaware and believe she is dating a more suitable boy. My information comes from the girl's friends. If the boot were on the other foot, I would want to know. Do I speak up, or shut up?*

If the boot were on the other foot you'd want to know, would you? Well, that may be dandy enough, but imagine how life would be if we all assumed that others thought as we did? We'd all vote for the same political party; all spend our holidays visiting bars in Bangkok where young women pop table-tennis balls out of places you didn't know women had places; and we'd all be impatiently waiting for Mel Gibson's next movie (which, after his Aramaic-dialogue *The Passion of The Christ*, turned out to be a film set against a backdrop of the Mayan empire and had a script spoken in an ancient dialect called Yucatec. What will he do next? Can you bear to wait? Well, can you?).

Let's overlook the fact that a girl's friends are not always the most reliable sources of information; or that sources tend to be put in an awkward position when the prickly information that they've passed on becomes public knowledge, and is traced back to them. If you abuse this snippet of gossip, it may be the last snippet with which you're ever entrusted. The person you need to talk to is not the girl's mother, but the girl herself. If she sees nothing untoward in her relationship, encourage her to be open with her mother about it. After all, her mother will be able to alert her daughter to all the downsides of older men, being firmly hitched to one herself.

Form a queue, boys

I have had so many one-night stands that friends consider me promiscuous. Several of my partners were dating another woman at the time. I feel no guilt; sex is something to be enjoyed between two people. Should I feel bad because I feel no moral pangs?

The world is full of people who are ready to read it the wrong way when they see a woman regularly climbing in and out of other women's beds after having made love to these women's husbands and boyfriends behind their back (I mean in a figurative sense, not a *Kama Sutra* one).

Your frankness reminds me of the multiple-married Zsa Zsa Gabor who, asked how many husbands she'd had, answered: 'You mean apart from my own?' But just because you've had more hands up your skirt than Miss Piggy doesn't necessarily mean you are promiscuous. Who knows, you may think of yourself as someone working on Mother Nature's behalf to ensure that there is no danger of our becoming an endangered species. That sort of puts you in the same environmental bracket as David Bellamy and David Attenborough, doesn't it?

If your trysts were with unattached men, people might care less. By targeting already-hitched men, you are colluding in a betrayal and confecting the potential for pain and hurt. That rankles in most people's moral codes, even if they transgress those codes themselves.

One other thing: even if you don't have to adjust your behaviour, you should maybe nevertheless watch your language. Lauren Bacall can ask a waiter for a muffin and make it sound like she's inviting him to an orgy. And you? When you say you 'feel no moral pangs', you make them sound like spasms that might afflict women when they occasionally try to keep their thighs closed.

Man for rent

My girlfriend recently moved out of her parents' house into a flat. I am still based at home, living with my parents. Because I pay minimal rent at home, and because I will be spending a hefty chunk of my time at my girlfriend's flat, for which she pays everything, should I contribute to her rent?

Chipping in to a partner's rent is not a recipe for long-term harmony. It's tricky enough sharing your living space with someone with whom you've chosen to set up home. It is trickier still living under the same roof as someone with whom you're not yet sure you want to spend the rest of your life. Or, at any rate, with whom you want to cohabit until such time as your respective dieticians advise that your rival food intolerances render you incompatible – incompatible food intolerances being the new adultery ('You mean to tell me you eat gluten? And lactose products, too? Get out of my sight, and shut the door behind you! You sicken me!').

Making a contribution to your girlfriend's rent is like putting a down-payment on an item in a shop, with no commitment to buy. Just as the store cannot now sell that product to someone else, so your girlfriend may feel that she has lost the right – in her own flat! – to get so mad at you that she can tell you to leave; because you can always remind her that you pay a slice of her rent, giving you at least some right to stay and make yourself comfortable.

Your girlfriend moved out of her parents' house having first calculated whether she could afford to rent her own flat, regardless of the future of your relationship. Otherwise, she would have asked you in advance to make a contribution to her rent. It would be emotionally fairer on her if you balanced the books by keeping the fridge well stocked and buying theatre tickets.

Speed freak

Although happily attached, with no desire to stray, I love the idea of going speed-dating, simply to meet new people, have fun, and make new friends. A male friend says it would be wrong to do it, even if I made it clear that all I wanted was friendship, and even if my fella doesn't mind. Is my friend right?

Let's summarise what we have so far: you're happily attached to a broad-minded boyfriend, and you have no desire to stray. Yet you yearn to spend an evening chatting briefly to several strange men – each of whom, in turn, will be nursing the impression that they could spend more time with you if they happen to play their cards right. A bit like an emotional lap-dancer, then.

Is your friend right? Yes, he is. He can imagine how he might feel were he one of the men you were speed-dating on your fun night out. If he didn't care for the sight of you, then he wouldn't be too bothered what your motives were for being there. But then he probably wouldn't want to see you again as a friend, either.

If he did take to you, he'd be cheesed off to hear that you were a window-display model only: this, equally, might irritate him enough to want never to see you again. I'm not sure where the fun, or new friends, would enter this equation.

Still can't see the problem? Then imagine being inter-viewed for an appealing job, only to be told as you're leaving that the interviewer isn't actually looking for an employee, just new friends.

As for your being happily attached, with no desire to stray, you sound like someone who has just bought a great outfit for a big party, but continues window-shopping with the receipt in your purse just in case you spot something more dazzling before the actual event.

Stand by your own man

A gay friend, Clive, flirts with my boyfriend, hugging him tightly when we leave the pub. A mutual friend confirmed that Clive fancies my boyfriend, who doesn't feel the same, but doesn't want to make a scene. Should I warn Clive off, or encourage my boyfriend to say something to Clive?

Maybe Clive has got the wrong end of the stick with regard to *Queer Eye for the Straight Guy* and hasn't realised that he's supposed only to reorganise your boyfriend's wardrobe and interior decor, not his sexuality. Or maybe Clive has picked up, on his sexual radar, that your man is not as averse as you think to a walk on the wild side.

Norman Mailer reckons that there probably isn't a sensitive heterosexual alive who isn't preoccupied with his latent homosexuality. Maybe, but I can't say I've noticed much such preoccupation in, say, Donald Rumsfeld (of course, Mailer is the novelist of whom a critic said that he would be fine 'if only he would take his eyes from the world's genital glands').

Warning Clive off, or openly challenging your boyfriend to renounce any feelings of homosexuality, latent or otherwise, is unlikely to resolve the problem in a satisfying way. If your boyfriend is old enough to go to a pub, he is doubtless also old enough to make his feelings clear to Clive without causing offence – assuming that he really does have absolutely no interest in canoodling with Clive. If Clive is as good a friend as you think he is, he will take defeat gracefully, without causing you or your boyfriend awkwardness or embarrassment.

Alternatively, befriend an attractive gay man and take him to the pub with you to divert Clive's attention. Don't play macho; play matchmaker.

Split decision

> **?** *My partner and I are moving in to a flat together. I earn three times as much as she does, so I thought I should pay three-quarters of the rent. Reluctantly, she agreed. I thought the same should also go for council tax and utility bills. Now we need furniture. Should we split this 75:25 as well? Where do we stop?*

What does your partner think? Having reluctantly agreed to the 75:25 split so far, is she, too, having doubts about now extending this regime to sofas and steaks?

Of course, a pure human spirit would not much care who paid for what, so long as all the bills were cleared and you were both happy. It's when the bliss begins to wane that financial friction might arise, becoming a sort of continuation of estrangement by other means.

When you're splitting the bill in a restaurant with friends, and someone orders lobster, nobody minds. It evens out: some drank more, the person who had only a salad swallowed two puddings. But do you feel as magnanimous if the lobster-orderer is a relative stranger?

You have shown great generosity, which your partner has accepted with grace. Push it much further and you risk one day resenting the arrangement. She, meanwhile, may begin to feel as though she is inescapably in your debt. You could always chip in more informally, by picking up restaurant bills, or paying for cinema tickets.

In *The Threepenny Opera* Brecht says that 'a man who sees another man on the street corner with only a stump for an arm will be so shocked the first time he'll give him sixpence. But the second time it'll be only a threepenny bit. And if he sees him a third time he'll cold-bloodedly have him handed over to the police.' Odd thing, human nature.

Mail merging

? *My friend uses an internet dating site and exchanged e-mails with a man who said he had been widowed. They met several times and made love. We then learnt that he has a wife who is alive and well. I think the wife should be told but my friend does not. Who is right?*

The injured party is not your friend, but the man's wife. And it's certainly not you. Whether your friend prefers to keep the wife in the dark because she feels that poking her nose into someone else's marriage will do little to help the wife, or is keeping her distance because she suspected this fellow's story but went ahead and slept with him anyway, she is probably doing the right thing.

Anyway, you don't suggest that your friend is heartbroken or distraught as a result of the encounter. Her concern from the start has always been not to hurt others.

Who knows what kind of relationship this man and his wife have? What if he has his own Clinton-style tariff of what does and doesn't constitute sexual relations, and in his book a one-night stand with an internet date is no more adulterous than having an intern ferreting under your desk in the Oval Office? Maybe the man's wife already knows (do you suppose Jackie Kennedy had no idea what JFK was getting up to?). Maybe the wife gets her kicks elsewhere, too? And if she doesn't, how would you go about judging whether your friend, having just bedded the husband, would be doing the wife a favour by bringing her husband's infidelity to her attention?

If this is your friend's first internet date, she should consider herself lucky that the man actually turned out to be all he said he was, bar a widower. She should try a little more caution next time. Remember what Mae West said: 'Give a man a free hand and he'll run it all over you.'

I'm not in Love

? *I am twenty-two and have been going out with my twenty-four-year-old girlfriend for six months. Though I really like her, I don't love her, and there is no chance that she will be the one with whom I settle down. Am I being fair to her? She might miss out on a man who could love her fully in future.*

Let me guess: do you also, say, own a rusty old jalopy in which you're quite happy pootling around town – although you know, in your heart, that you're the sort of guy who will one day be the proud owner of a Maserati?

How do you know your girlfriend won't grow on you? Have you never seen one of those Hollywood movies – you know, those romantic comedies with Meg Ryan, Audrey Hepburn or Cary Grant – in which a man and woman begin by getting on so badly that they'd only ever want to look directly at each other if they were trying to cure their hiccups, but end up swimming dreamily in each other's eyes?

Frankly, six months seems a long time to be dating someone for whom you apparently have so little passion that you can already envisage the day when you'll be heading your separate ways. You can stumble across more romantic-sounding relationships even among the sort of men who don't talk to their date because they're saving their breath so that they can inflate her later in the evening.

If your girlfriend is old enough to be dating you, then – if you explain honestly how you feel about the unlikelihood of your ever drawing your pensions together – she is also old enough to decide for herself whether it's a relationship she wants to pursue. Anyway, who says she isn't sticking around just for as long as it takes her to find a man who truly loves her?

2 Family Ties
(you down)

'Happiness is having a large, loving, caring, close-knit family in another city'

George Burns

Liquor Licence

? *My sixteen-year-old son has begun going to pubs with his friends. As it is illegal for him to buy alcohol, should I carry on letting him go, or do I stop him?*

Some people think that drinking when under age is wrong. These people are called the police.

As to what counts as under age, that varies. In some countries you can drink at an age at which you still can't vote. In others, you can vote but not yet legally drink. Some countries have very restrictive rules on drinking; some have very restrictive rules on voting (often these are the same countries). In America, as a young man you may go abroad and kill for your country but may not console yourself when you get home from war with anything more intoxicating than a Pepsi. In France, nobody minds much if children move almost directly from breast milk to watered-down burgundy.

In England children are not allowed to drink alcohol in pubs, yet are encouraged to eat the pub's children's meal of chicken nuggets made from a farmer's old underpants minced up with chicken skin, rolled in breadcrumbs and deep-fried. Confused? So is your son, probably.

Rabbit punch

I bought pet rabbits for my daughters: two, for company, and brothers, so they would not fight. But they did, so I took them to be neutered: £50 each. Next came teeth problems: £76 and £95 to sort out. These are only rabbits! They cost £20 to buy! Special hay costs me £8 a kilo! A family in Africa could live for weeks on this kind of money. Deep down I think it is not right.

It's true that vet fees can be as alarming as finding out that the woman you've been chatting up at the bar is Mike Tyson's new girlfriend. You drop off a poorly rabbit for a minor surgical procedure and pick it up the next day to find that it has run up an overnight bill that suggests it emptied the mini-bar of champagne and macadamia nuts before staying up all night watching the pay-per-view porn channel (and being unimpressed by the prolific bedroom work rate of the lead actors because, well, because it's a rabbit). Either that or it ran up a string of losses by placing telephone bets with a bookie on races at the dog track, as a result of believing that being a rabbit gives it a special insight into greyhound behaviour.

Getting a sick pet treated by a vet makes, in financial terms, about as much sense as getting a pencil repaired: it's cheaper to get a new one. You know when you buy a £1.99 torch and the salesman tries to sell you a three-year warranty for £17.50, and you snort at his loopy arithmetic? Well, that's pretty much how pet medical insurance works. Pets are a sort of loss-leader for vets. It's like razor manufacturers selling you a razor for pennies to lock you in to having to buy its expensive blades for the rest of your shaving life.

But who looks at pets in purely financial terms? Ever thought of moving near a zoo? That might be cheaper.

White Lies

? *As lying is generally considered to be unethical, is it still right for me to tell my children that Father Christmas exists?*

When telling anyone anything, you have two options. You can tell them the truth, or you can tell lies. Some people think that lies are a very pale imitation of the truth, and therefore unsatisfactory, but until there is some other way of avoiding having to say what really happened, or what you really think, then lies are a handy makeshift alternative.

Many high-minded people believe that the truth is so valuable a commodity that it just cheapens it to use it profligately. It's like debasing the currency. That's why many believe that white lies don't do too much harm, providing, as Margot Asquith liked to say, you're not producing enough to ice a cake.

It's often the people who say they never lie who are the liars to steer clear of the most. Politicians have to lie, if only to keep some sort of national dialogue going ('national dialogue' being the parliamentary term for 'trying to provoke John Prescott to punch someone'). Lawyers, if they don't actually lie, have to at least believe the shameless lies told to them by the clients whom they are representing and who have sworn blind that they are innocent.

Nobody needs telling that Father Christmas does or doesn't exist. It just dawns on you as you grow older, like realising that maybe Joan Rivers has had a facelift. If your children are twenty-seven and still believe in Santa Claus, then, OK, go ahead and tell them.

Family planning

On a genealogy website I noticed a contributor claiming descent from my rich and influential forebears, which I knew to be untrue. He was clearly pleased to be linked to them. If accepted by other researchers, incorrect information would prevail.

For those of us who can trace our family meticulously all the way back to . . . let's see . . . our, yes, our great-grandparents, the new obsession with genealogy can feel a little nerdy. And everyone loses the trail sooner or later.

Mapping your ancestors is like tracing your path through a giant maze, turning right and left until you're stumped about which way next to turn. Nobody's ever succeeded in reaching the centre of the maze and whooping, 'I made it! I traced my family right back to Adam and Eve!' (the parallels between mazes and genealogy go further. You know those cul-de-sacs you hit in mazes? Well, they represent moments in history when frenetic in-breeding resulted in family trees turning back on themselves. And those holes in maze hedges? That's where people tracing their ancestry discovered that they were distantly related to Dan Quayle and made a dive into an alternative genealogical path).

How much difference does it make who your forebears were, anyway?

Whenever you see seventeenth-century portraits of people's ancestors, they all look identical. Maybe the same painter was churning out stock portraits, customised with a bigger nose, or a higher forehead, just before delivery – like a tailor shortening the trouser hems on an off-the-peg suit. Or maybe everyone in the seventeenth century really did look similar on account of in-breeding.

You want to chase off the impostor? Trace your family line back to Dan Quayle's. That should send him scurrying for an alternative family tree to hang from.

Private View

My twenty-one-year-old daughter is backpacking in Asia. Soon after her leaving (and going out of contact for several days), a letter arrived, addressed to her. It gave the appearance of a letter requiring immediate action. I opened it and took the action required. Should I have done so without her permission, or did I invade her privacy?

How exactly did this envelope give 'the appearance of a letter requiring immediate action'? Was it stamped 'URGENT', like those letters from estate agents informing you that they've just sold a house in your street for an eye-popping price and they have a very disappointed underbidder who would pay 20 per cent over the market rate for your very similar property (but who may prove to be strangely elusive if you respond to the letter)?

A twenty-one-year-old is old enough to let it be known what she might want done on her behalf while she's backpacking around Asia. Had your daughter wanted her non-personal mail opened, she would have said as much before leaving. If it should turn out that she erred in not making such an arrangement before departing, then she'll know better next time. It's part of growing up and learning from your mistakes.

In any case, non-personal mail can usually wait. She was out of contact for only a few days. People go on holiday for a fortnight without employing someone to check their mail daily for correspondence which gives 'the appearance of a letter requiring immediate action'.

As a parent, you behaved nosily under the camouflage of behaving helpfully. Anyway, answering letters is very unoriginal. Responding to letters from people who haven't yet sent them to you always produces far more entertaining results.

Boiler suit chic

> **?** *My wife (early forties), has given up wearing fashionable, attractive clothes, settling on what I call the 'East German Tractor Factory Look'. Should I be pleased she is not spending the family income on frivolous fashion, or mourn her loss of desire to appeal?*

When we eat food that's past its sell-by date we risk hurting only ourselves. When we wear clothes that are past their sell-by date we risk not only hurting ourselves, but upsetting others, too. Yet food comes labelled with health advice, cooking instructions and serving suggestions, while clothes come with nothing. If clothes labels resembled food labels more, middle-aged men would know not to wear school rugby shirts as casual weekend wear, because a label inside would read: 'Best before 1982. Aesthetic warning: wear on sports fields only.'

East German factory wear, it's true, isn't too appealing. But if you saw Charlize Theron in a boiler suit, would you think her unattractive? Now, lest this prompt you to suggest to your wife that factory wear really suits Theron, but not her, think twice. Women who seek a man's opinion on clothes are keen for him to be frank, and will react philosophically whether he answers 'You look fabulous in that' or 'Wow! That really suits you!' Beyond that, anything is risky.

Instead, buy your wife a glamorous outfit (no, not from a Soho porn shop), and she'll get the message that you still think she's a hot little biscuit. She'll say: 'Why didn't you just say straight out that you didn't like me in boiler suits?' It's a trick question. Don't answer it.

Bosom buddies

? *On his return from a sleepover at a school friend's house, our eight-year-old son said he'd seen – unsupervised – a film about zombie flesh-eaters and another involving 'four ladies in just their pants rubbing their bosoms'; presumably soft-core porn. It's possible that the boy's parents are unaware that their son watches such stuff. Should we tell them, or just keep our son away?*

Obviously, there are important questions to be asked in such a situation – most pressingly, did he happen to mention the name of that film with the 'four ladies in just their pants rubbing their bosoms', and whether it was available in most video rental shops?

You evidently found it distressing that your son was exposed, at so tender an age, to images that either corrupted him, or wastefully went way over his head: either way, you're upset. But cloistering him at home until you think he has reached an age when it is safe to let him loose in the ugly world outside your front door may not be the healthiest option.

Casually mentioning the episode to the child's parents would alert them to a potential problem in their boy's viewing habits and give them the opportunity to do something about it, assuming that they wished to do something. But because it is unlikely that your son's school friend brought the bosom-rubbing video into his house, it must belong to the parents. That they left the tape within easy reach of their own son seems to suggest that they have a fairly relaxed attitude to such matters. Of course, it may make your intervention that much more delicate if the video had not been hired from a rental shop but was home-made by the school friend's parents for their own entertainment.

Teething trouble

I recommended my dentist to my daughter's boyfriend. Recently, my daughter revealed that the bill was unpaid, but said: 'Don't worry, debt collectors have bought the unpaid bill, so the dentist has still got his money.' How can I persuade this man (who is twenty-eight) and my daughter (twenty) that he behaved unethically?

Why are people always so keen to recommend their dentists and their doctors, anyway? Do you suppose dentists behave the same way in reverse, recommending their favourite patients to other professionals ('If you're looking for a reliable client, I can really recommend John Smith. Never queries the bill. Always pays on time. Mention my name when you invoice him.').

Dentists move in mysterious ways. Whichever dentist you visit, and however many times he's seen you before, he always takes fresh X-rays before deciding what needs doing. Why is that, when air crash investigators can look at a set of teeth and tell you how many GCSEs their owner had, his credit rating, and whether he'd ever been engaged to Jennifer Lopez?

But just because a dentist has insurance against non-paying patients, that doesn't mean your daughter's boyfriend can selfishly milk that loophole. If we all behaved as he did then premiums for whichever policy it is that dentists take out to cover themselves for bill-defaulters would balloon; and our dentistry bills would rise accordingly – cash upfront.

Not that I'm clear how the debt collectors who bought the unpaid bill will be recovering their outlay. Maybe via a late-night visit to your daughter's boyfriend. If after their visit he requires emergency knee surgery, perhaps he'll again look to you for a recommendation.

Hear no evil

? *My nephew is selling his house because of noisy neighbours. Wary of jeopardising the sale price, he has resorted to underhand methods to ensure buyers remain ignorant of the nuisance. Should I say something?*

Should you say something? Possibly. Though, obviously, not too loudly; not from inside the neighbours' house; not when a prospective buyer is nosing around your nephew's property.

When it comes to property transactions, the onus is still largely on the buyer to establish whether a house is structurally sound and worth the asking price, the basic guiding principle being *caveat emptor* (literally, 'Would this beat living in an empty cave?'). It falls to a buyer to hire a surveyor to scrutinise the building with that profession's trademark thoroughness ('Having been refused permission by the owners to lift floorboards and hack open plastered walls, I am unable to comment on the state of the property's wiring'); also to get his lawyer to investigate whether the council has approved the siting of a nuclear waste dump at the end of the street (though there is still no way of protecting yourself from the possibility of Mick Hucknall moving in next door).

If your nephew has had prickly relations with his neighbours, whether over noise or other issues, his lawyer may advise him that not revealing as much could leave him open to future compensation claims from whoever buys his property. Should his lawyer advise that the nuisance is one that does not, legally, require confessing, your nephew might feel he may keep silent, thereby enabling him, once he has moved, to sleep more peacefully at night: though maybe not in a moral sense.

Not so fine behaviour

I asked my eighteen-year-old daughter to do an errand for me. She agreed, but came back with a parking ticket. She feels I should pay, as she was doing me a favour. I feel she should have been more careful and parked in the pay-and-display bays near by.

Get your daughter to answer this questionnaire, answering 'agree' or 'disagree' in each case:

1. My mother asked me to pass her a knife. So I tossed a knife in her direction. Unfortunately it embedded itself in her arm, requiring major surgery. But it was her fault, since if she hadn't asked me for a knife, I wouldn't have needed to throw one.

2. At a friend's house, realising there was no ashtray within reach, I stubbed out my cigarette on the carpet. My friend's mother is furious. But if only she'd bothered to leave out an ashtray, it wouldn't have happened, would it?

3. I asked my dad for money to buy a CD. I bought a *Coldplay* album. So my father is entirely to blame for my poor taste in music, right?

4. When I get drunk in a bar and feel ill the next day, I'm

justified in suing the barman for his thoughtlessness in continuing to serve me when he knew it might result in a hangover.

5. I voted Labour. But when I see the mess the country is in under Tony Blair I blame everything on the Tories for not urging me, during the general election, to 'Vote Tory' more forcefully than Tony Blair urged me to 'Vote Labour'.

And now get your daughter to answer this one:

6. When running an errand for my mother, I got a parking ticket. My mother should pay the parking fine, shouldn't she, because had I not been doing her a favour, I wouldn't have been put in the position where I might cause a parking offence?

Our Christmas pudding

My spinster sister-in-law alights on our family at Christmas, contributes nothing to the meals, receives presents but gives none, avoids washing-up, wants only to watch TV and will not join in any games. This will be the thirty-third year of this. I itch to be very rude, but this would spoil our family get-together and hurt my wife and in-laws. Am I being ungracious?

I think that you're forgetting one of the key messages of Christmas – an occasion that has become mired in commercialism but was designed to make us all appreciate why we choose to spend the rest of the year not seeing most of our relatives.

Of course, that is not the only purpose of gathering your extended family around a Christmas table heaving with enough food to feed a Florida cruise ship: another key purpose is trying to work out how farmers managed to breed a turkey with such unfeasibly disproportionate breasts without either using silicone implants or having to pay Dolly Parton a royalty fee.

On the bright side, if the worst happens in the hothouse heat of Christmas and you do let your frustrations loose by abusing a close relative, it's not as bad as letting your frustrations loose by unleashing a volley of abuse at a close colleague at a Christmas party: if you badmouth your sister-in-law, at least you won't have to start looking for a new job on Boxing Day.

But why not try W.C. Fields' trusted recipe for surviving Christmas with all the family? Fields found a way to make Christmas at his house at least six or seven times more pleasant than anywhere else. 'We start drinking early,' he explained. 'And while everyone else is seeing only one Santa Claus, we'll be seeing six or seven.'

Just pants!

? *My husband bought me underwear for my birthday which I quite liked, but it did not fit me. He said I could change it, which I did – for something different, which he now does not like. Should I keep my choice or go back to his original gift, even though I like it less and find it less comfortable?*

When you say your husband bought you underwear that did not fit, have you considered the possibility that he bought it for you in a size that he himself would be able to relax in when the mood takes him? Men are like this with presents, which is why they consider a cordless drill, or a *Black & Decker Workmate*, as suitable gifts for wives and girlfriends.

Men persist in buying women lingerie even though their track record shows them to be poor judges of buying underwear even for themselves. Men buy pants with luridly detailed messages to women inscribed across the crotch, as if women are so starved of reading matter that they rely on men's Y-fronts to keep them abreast of world news. Men, listen: if a woman has the time, and the inclination, to pause to read your underwear, then your underwear is not doing the job you maybe intended it to. Equally, if a woman is already bored by the idea of talking to you, she is not going to be interested in striking up a conversation with your Y-fronts.

It's true that it is traditionally the gift-giver who gets to choose the present, however much the recipient might hate it. That's the tradition we call Christmas. But having said you could change the underwear, your husband should now be glad that the gift he bought you is giving you the pleasure he hoped for. Maybe you could meet him halfway: keep the replacement underwear, but occasionally pin Post-It Note messages on to the crotch.

Party politics

Though we are on a modest income, it has always been our ambition to send our child through private school. We are just about managing with the fees, but we have a zero social budget. Other pupils have elaborate, expensive birthday parties, inviting everyone in the class. Is it wrong for us to let our child attend, knowing that we are unable to reciprocate in as grand a manner?

Actually, there's no law requiring you to reciprocate at all.

Sometimes it's best not to. There are many 'friendships' that have lasted for decades purely because two couples have felt endlessly obliged to repay a dinner invitation, even though each couple knows that they dislike each other – but dislike being thought rude even more.

Take a leaf out of the Queen's book. She still invites thousands of people every year to parties in her garden, even though she hardly ever gets invited back to their place. Don't take your cue from Adolf Hitler, who made a habit of turning up on neighbouring countries' doorsteps uninvited and organising his own surprise party. (There are probably postgraduate students writing theses on how the comparative histories of Britain and Germany in the early twentieth century can be explained by means of their respective party-invitation etiquette.) Children like getting presents, but they don't much care who is throwing the party. I doubt that the school friends are keeping count. And if any are the type who are, then why would you care for their opinion?

Don't let your child feel embarrassed. There will be time enough for that later, when they go to the office party and embarrass themselves so much that they wake the next morning wanting to enrol in a witness-protection programme.

Bonus issue

I work part-time and recently received, out of the blue, £200 as a bonus. We have three teenage children and are, thanks to my husband's income, comfortably off. I want to give this windfall to charity, but my husband thinks I should spend it on a treat for the family. I feel this is my money. On the other hand, I rely on my husband's monthly cheques.

The division of money in a marriage can be as tricky as the division of labour, and it is true that husband and wife do not always see things the same way. A husband's definition of the word 'mess', for instance, is often very different from that of his wife. Men are able to manoeuvre themselves around piles of old newspapers, dirty laundry, toys and bags of old clothes waiting to be taken to a charity shop, whereas women – who may lack the physical agility to do this – are more likely to screech in frustration about how the house has become a tip.

'Necessity' is another word that can divide the sexes. To a wife, necessities are such things as food, shelter and clothes for the children, whereas to a man a necessity might be a new home cinema system, which might look just like the one he bought four months ago but which is jam-packed with enhancements that his wife is unable to notice on account of having to use all her powers of concentration to manoeuvre around the old newspapers, dirty laundry and toys.

Pooling income in a marriage does not mean that each partner cannot occasionally indulge themselves – family finances permitting. So you should not feel guilty about spending your windfall how you wish, particularly given that you want to donate it to charity – although that doesn't necessarily preclude reserving a small portion of the bonus for a family treat.

Movie tone

> **?** *I used my aunt's e-mail contact list (from an e-mail she sent me) to send a message recommending a film. I knew some of the recipients, but not others. Some complained about my e-mail – even though I wasn't trying to sell anything, wasn't advocating something political, and I'm the nephew of someone everyone on that list knows, so it's not spam. Isn't this harsh?*

What an intriguing query. So intriguing, in fact, that I forwarded your e-mail to everyone on my own e-mail address book and urged all of them – since the e-mail was not spam – to forward it to everyone on their address list, too. With luck, you might now receive responses to your dilemma from interested correspondents across the globe. Who knows? Some of them might even suggest that the surest route to resolving your dilemma lies in buying an ointment that can 'increase your P*n!$ s)zE. M_ake hEr hAppY. Guar'ntE_d LOw pr;ces'.

Actually, I didn't forward your e-mail. For all, bar those addicted to their BlackBerries, it's tricky enough coping with being exposed to mobile phone calls and e-mails around the clock, wherever you might happen to be in the world, from people you actually know and might wish to hear from, without also becoming vulnerable to a similar bombardment from strangers.

You have no more right to inflict your unsolicited e-mail on people who are known to your aunt, but who are utter strangers to you (and, more crucially, you to them), than you would have to knock on the front doors of these strangers and, uninvited, join them for dinner. Unless you are a renowned film critic, your aunt's acquaintances will be as hungry to hear your views of new films as they would be to watch a Kevin Costner movie unsedated.

Not fit for marriage

I am struggling to find a dress for a wedding. At my mother's invitation, I sent her my measurements. She has gone to great trouble to find me a silk dress from a shop that doesn't take returns. It fits reasonably well, but I don't like it. Is it my mother's problem or mine?

It's not as if you're Zsa Zsa Gabor or Elizabeth Taylor: you'll be wearing the dress only the once. If you hate it so much that you can't bear to wear it at all, you could always just keep it for some other use. You could turn it into cushion covers, for instance, or start going to fancy dress parties as Miss Havisham. Or you could put it in your lavatory to discreetly hide a giant toilet roll, the way people hide lavatory paper under the skirts of flamenco-dancer dolls.

What you can't do is stick your mother for the money. 'At my mother's invitation' sounds like a weasel's way of shifting the blame on to your ma; like sliding the tablecloth a little, so that it looks as if it was your neighbour who spilt their soup so clumsily. If you've grown out of having your mother spit on her hankie to wipe chocolate stains from around your mouth, you should also have stopped doing things because your mother suggested them; otherwise you might not even be marrying the man you've chosen (YOU: 'Mum, we're planning to have a civil ceremony.' YOUR MOTHER: 'Then why are you marrying *him*!').

If there were any chance of your not sharing your mother's taste in wedding dresses, you should never have divulged your measurements. By doing so, you have entered into a pact whereby you gave her licence to shop on your behalf. It is unfortunate, but it is also your burden to rid yourself of your unwanted dress.

You could always sell it to Elizabeth Taylor.

Game theory

? *My younger brother, who is twelve, persuaded my mother to buy him a video game that is unsuitable for his age: it is not only violent, but includes pornographic content – a strict no-no in my family. The problem is that my brother didn't tell my parents about the game's contents before they bought it. I am torn: should I spill the beans to my parents or be loyal to my brother?*

There are four reasons to intervene in your younger brother's video gaming habits:

(1) because he lied to your parents, procuring his new video game by deceit;

(2) because, whatever he himself might think, a twelve-year-old is not emotionally mature enough to handle adult porn;

(3) because he won't let you play with his video game and you're jealous; and

(4) because, being protective of your brother, you don't want him growing up believing that every woman in the non-cyber world also likes to plunge into frenzied sex with any pizza-delivery boy and pool-repair man who rings her doorbell, while contorting her face into expressions of such apparent agony that a more considerate partner than a passing poolman might be prompted to inquire whether she was troubled by trapped wind.

Had you immersed yourself in your brother's morally dubious video game you might have stumbled upon the possibility that – between (on the one hand) telling your parents, and (on the other hand) not grassing up your sibling – there is a happy, but also morally dubious, medium: blackmail. Blackmail enables you to confiscate your brother's video game in return for promising not to squeal to your parents about how he lied to them. This resolves your ethical concerns, but without any recrimination at the family dinner table.

Family Service

We have teenage children, and both of us work. As parents, are we morally obliged, as they think we are, to wait on them: cleaning, cooking, laundering clothes, taking criticism and abuse when we don't meet their expectations? Or is our moral duty to teach them how to handle household chores, so that they do not lack the basic skills they will need in adulthood?

A teenager would answer this question differently from the way in which a parent would; assuming that you can get a teenager to give any kind of answer. Teenagers have different priorities. To them, the important things in life are saving the world from capitalism, protecting the polar ice caps and ending world poverty. To an adult, a major goal can be getting up from the sofa and being able to remember what it is they stood up to do.

Children see it as a parent's duty to protect and feed them until they reach adulthood. They have watched too many natural-history documentaries, which show doting parental wildlife tirelessly hunting for food for their young to ensure the survival of the species – while overlooking the fact that the parents on nature programmes are not also obliged to hold down a day job to keep their young in the correct brand of trainers.

As a parent, you certainly have a duty to feed, nurse and care for your children (although not, in the manner of some Italian sons, until they are old enough to have their own grown-up sons). But it is also your duty to give your children a taste of what life holds in store. So find a compromise. Sometimes the only thing that comforts parents through the trials of living with teenage children is knowing that they might one day have teenagers of their own.

Cinema Scope

My fourteen-year-old son and some of his school chums have been to the local cinema to see movies such as Borat, *which are rated 15. As a law-abiding and loving parent, should I stop my son from going with his friends to see such movies? Should I also warn the cinema if I am aware that his school friends are planning a trip?*

Most people regard the age ratings on movies not so much as one of the Ten Commandments, more as the cinematic equivalent of those 'serving suggestions' that food manufacturers depict on the labels of their cans.

Yes, in an ideal world you would serve your hoummos spread out on a rustic dish, drizzled in olive oil, with a few black olives on the side and a sprinkle of chopped coriander on top: in practice, you eat the hoummos straight from the pack, scraping it on to shards of stale pitta bread while standing over the sink to save dirtying any plates.

Unless a movie is really not suitable for a minor (anything disturbing, such as violent Quentin Tarantino films; or seeing Jennifer Lopez in *Gigli*), it is a rite of youth to sneak into films from which you are technically excluded. Your son is entering the only phase in his life where he will actually enjoy 18-rated movies, a period that will last fifteen years or so. After the age of thirty, an 18-rating is more commonly a signal that a film is too violent, too scary, or too highbrow to make for jolly Saturday-night entertainment, and you seek out the nearest screening of *It's A Wonderful Life* instead.

Even actors tire of 18-rated movies. The biggest contribution Arnold Schwarzenegger made to movies was when he stopped making them and diverted his efforts to politics; which pleased his leading ladies, who always hated playing alongside a man whose breasts were bigger than their own.

Sound of Silence

I bought my parents expensive portable music players for their birthdays, which they can use with a computer. Unfortunately, the devices do not work with their home PC, prompting them to update their computer for use with both their new music players and other new technology. Should I contribute to the cost of the upgrade because my gift forced their hand?

Today anything you buy for your home that has a plug attached to it is designed to communicate with other devices as part of an integrated home network. A consumer electronics wizard must have decided that what we all yearn for is a fridge that, when you remove a bottle of champagne, automatically triggers the lights to dim, the electronic window shutters to close and the music centre to play something slow and smoochy. This is because the fridge has calculated that you are planning to seduce a woman you've just brought home.

Actually, the reason you removed the champagne is that it was blocking access to the fridge's computer panel, which a technician has come to fix on account of its constant malfunctioning (a technician now growing nervous that you are planning to make a pass at him).

The trouble is that though all these devices communicate, they don't all speak the same language. Our houses have become electronic Towers of Babel, resulting in: (1) food blenders that always know when your bath wants to be filled with carrot juice; and (2) technicians who charge £270 to show you how to plug in your new audio-compatible toaster.

Your parents are in a jam as a result of your well-meant, but ill-researched, generosity. They don't have to link their music players to a computer. If they wish to, it's a matter, and a cost, for them.

Auto cross

My father-in-law lent me his car (he also has a company car), which I agreed to insure, tax and maintain. Now an MoT shows it needs £1,000 of work (it is worth only £2,000). He expects me to foot this bill, even though he did 20,000 miles in it last year, against my mere 1,000 miles to date. Should I pay up? His argument is that £1,000 is cheaper than my buying a car.

In-laws are one of those gambles in marriage. You never know what might turn up. It's like a dish on a menu that reads 'comes garnished': you don't know whether your sirloin will arrive with lovely fat chips; with a twee sliver of mango; or with a tangle of whichever vegetables happened to be within the chef's reach, making your plate look as if Jackson Pollock is working in the kitchen.

To lend you his car was generous of your father-in-law. But generosity counts for less if it comes attached to so many strings that it becomes burdensome. It might be fair that you pay for running repairs, but it seems less fair to saddle you with the bill for remedying historic decay to make the car roadworthy. If you lend someone a cashmere sweater and they singe it on a barbecue, you might expect the contrite borrower to offer a replacement. What your in-law is proposing is more like lending someone a shampoo bottle with a spoonful of liquid left at the bottom and being affronted when they return it to you empty.

Maybe you did something to upset your father-in-law. Like marrying his daughter.

Missed payments

As a new mum I sometimes place items on my baby's buggy and leave a shop having forgotten to pay. If I'm still near the shop, I return and pay. Equally, if a food item I've ordered is omitted from my restaurant bill, I alert the restaurant because I feel that otherwise it's stealing. But my partner says that it's the fault of the shops/restaurants, so why draw their attention to it. Who's right?

It is a common complaint among mothers that childbirth seems to play havoc with their memory. Who knows? Maybe this is the result of vital brain-memory particles seeping into the placenta during the months of pregnancy. If only scientists could figure out how to decode the memories stored in them, placentas could serve as a collective computer-style data bank, a back-up repository of missed appointments, forgotten conversations and uncollected dry cleaning.

Men's memory function is also affected by childbirth, though in different ways. (Wife: 'I'm popping out, so you're in charge of all three kids till I get back.' Husband: 'Three?') Everyone may occasionally stray, even Winona Ryder, who walked out of a department store with goods that didn't belong to her; or George Bush who, Al Gore believes, walked off with a bunch of Florida ballots that didn't belong to him. To err may be human (and Mae West may have thought it felt divine), but you've got to pay your bills. Shops and restaurants employ security guards and install CCTV cameras to catch those who have been dishonest enough to leave without having settled up.

Paying for goods is not the retail equivalent of a game of tag. It is not the shop or café's responsibility to catch you. It's your responsibility to pay. Whatever your partner thinks. And don't forget it.

Present imperfect

My sister-in-law and I have agreed to spend a maximum of £15 on each other's children at Christmas. As her identical gifts to my two children this year were inappropriate, I returned them to the shop, only to discover that they'd been bought in a sale last summer and were worth only £1 each. Do I expose her? Continue spending £15 a child? Or play her at her own game?

You might think that your sister-in-law should have used the bonus of shopping in a sale to spend £15 a child, but on buying each child an item that had been knocked down from maybe £30, thereby passing on to them the benefit of the sale discount. Your sister-in-law, though, might think that she should accrue the benefit of being organised enough to plan her Christmas shopping so well in advance.

What if the presents your children received had not been 'inappropriate'? Presumably, you would have considered them to be worth £15, because you had assumed that was their original price. So what now bugs you? That your sister-in-law is £14 a child in profit?

And what bearing does price have on the value of the gift, exactly? There is a painting of sunflowers by Van Gogh which is worth millions, if genuine; but little if not by Vincent, as some art experts believe. Yet it is the same painting. People's perception of its creator's genius is being dictated by its price tag, whereas price is more usually dictated by a work's quality.

What if your sister-in-law found the perfect gift in an antiques shop for £15? Should she pay the ticket price, even though she knows that the shop owner would take £10, just to meet your rules? Perhaps your sister-in-law behaved not unethically but merely stingily. Which is sometimes worse.

Top pay

My twenty-four-year-old daughter stored her sports car's hard top in my garage over the summer. On going to refit it for the winter, we found it badly scored. My son's golf clubs had been removed from behind the top, so he is the prime suspect. But he denies having gone near it. Respraying the top cost £80, which my daughter and son refuse to pay. It was in my garage, so should I pay?

Oh, my, there's a jolly, give-and-take family setup. Do you ever play Monopoly together? Does it always end up with neighbours having to call the police? Or only sometimes?

You should pay the £80 as a paternal, peacekeeping gesture, on the understanding that – because the scratch was not your doing and you don't intend to be made a patsy twice – your daughter stores her hard top and your son his golf clubs elsewhere from now on. That might concentrate their minds.

Since you were not charging storage, you might feel that your generosity towards your daughter and son has been cruelly repaid not with thanks, but churlishness. Then again, having agreed to oversee storage, you were under some obligation to do your best to see that these items weren't carelessly, or negligently, mistreated. Having presumably done precisely this, it is naturally galling that the prime suspect denies having been anywhere near the hard top; in which case, if he can explain how he managed to extricate his golf clubs from behind the hard top without going anywhere near it, he might win a spot on Siegfried and Roy's magic show in Las Vegas. You, your daughter, even readers of this book, might be convinced that your son is responsible, but justice doesn't always work that way. Look at OJ Simpson.

Baby grand?

In reports about women delaying childbirth, or forgoing it altogether, such women are often portrayed as selfish. But what about the broader impact of population growth on our planet? Surely having children just to solve the pensions crisis, so that we have an excuse to slow down immigration, is selfish in itself? What is the ethical number of children to have, if any?

How many? That depends. Some religions would say as many as Nature (and God) blesses you with. Others would say that the right number is that which generates a population mix that allows the older members of society to raise the younger, and the younger to reach maturity in time to care for those who raised them; in an endless, virtuous cycle.

Others would argue that you should have only as many children as you can afford to raise, so that you are not a burden on fellow-taxpayers. Others say that it's not a personal balance sheet that you need to draw up but a global one; that we should bring into the world only as many children as the planet and our lifestyles can support without bequeathing a legacy of environmental havoc. These various moral calculations do not even begin to count those ugly societies that toy with eugenics to limit numbers.

Child-rearing has an ethical element, but no easy ethical yardstick by which to judge another's choices and actions. Partly this is because baby production is so effortless. It's Nature's equivalent of a *Blue Peter* craft-model demonstration: if you're bored on a Sunday afternoon, you can make your own baby just using odds and ends that you can lay your hands on without leaving the sofa. Even sticky tape isn't vital; although obviously it spices things up.

Just Log off

Without asking, a relative always makes use of my computer when staying with us, even though I have often asked him not to, even though my computer is not in a 'public' room and even though he brings his own, anyway. I find this behaviour intrusive.

There are considerate house guests and there are those who don't know where to draw the line. There are house guests who, when you tell them to help themselves to anything, still nibble your pistachios as shyly as someone who's been stung £6.75 once too often for a handful of nuts from a hotel minibar. And there are guests to whom you welcomingly say 'My house is your house', only to return from work to find that they've taken you at your word and sold it.

The danger with letting a stranger loose on your computer is that they could be typing in really embarrassing internet searches, such as 'gay porn', 'sex with llamas' or 'Mick Hucknall fan club'. These things will lodge, incriminatingly, for ever in your hard drive.

Crucially, you don't know whether the visitor has imported a debilitating bug that will require you to phone your computer helpline and join a queue ('Your position is: No 624'), some of whose members have been on hold so long that they have queries about software programs that became obsolete before the twelve-year-old who will eventually answer the phone was even born.

Next time your relative behaves this thoughtlessly, do this: when he's left the computer, log on to a 'sex with llamas' website and wait for a house member to stumble on it and point an accusing finger at the chap. If that fails to embarrass him, raise the shame quotient by faking his electronic fingerprints on the Mick Hucknall fan club site.

Dead Letters

I send birthday and Christmas presents to the grandson of a distant relative, because the boy's grandmother sent my own son presents until he turned twenty. After four years of receiving no letter of thanks, I began sending cheques instead: still no acknowledgement, although I can see that they've been cashed. Should I stop sending presents? I'd rather give the money to charity.

Yes, it's always slightly disheartening when you put yourself out to do something to give pleasure to someone and they respond by going around acting like nothing ever happened – no, wait! – I was thinking of Monica Lewinsky's plight with Bill Clinton, not yours.

By switching to sending cheques, you now at least know that your gift has arrived.

Seeing the debit on your statement is the banking equivalent of those e-mail systems that inform you when a message you sent has been read by its recipient.

Your heart may not be in it, but you are behaving well in repaying what you consider to be a notional debt to your relative's grandson. That the boy, or his mother, does not acknowledge your generosity may be graceless, but another's discourtesy is not sufficient moral grounds to behave badly in turn. Otherwise we'd enter a downward spiral that would end with us all talking to each other the way you might talk to a waiter who's just spilt soup in your lap.

If you would rather give the money to charity, there is a way both to eat your cake and have it. Many charities now run gift schemes whereby you send someone a card telling them you've bought them a present of, say, fifteen chickens for a village in Sri Lanka, or textbooks for a school in Kenya. Or

else, just send the boy stationery and see whether his family
takes the hint.

Midnight Son

*On leaving my brother to babysit my son, I casually
mentioned that I didn't think I'd be very late. But I
didn't come home until midnight (not that late for a
Saturday night). My brother says that I had a moral duty
to tell him that I would be home later than suggested –
although he hadn't asked me to return by a certain time.*

It's true that men often approach babysitting differently from
women. What especially foxes men is how, when babysitting,
the passage of time alters in a way that Stephen Hawking never
mentioned. You can lie on the sofa watching Australia's cricket
team hammer England into the ground as if they were burying
a tent peg and the next time you check your watch six hours
have passed. When babysitting, a man will engage the child in
every game he has played since his own childhood,
interspersed with tricks he has learnt using lit cigarettes, while
filling any slack periods by telling jokes that he wouldn't dare
repeat to any human old enough to understand English and/or
human reproduction. Then, exhausted but smugly proud of his
efforts, the man glances at his watch to see that *A FULL
SEVEN MINUTES HAVE ELAPSED*. That makes a clock-
watcher of any man.

But did you behave immorally? I'd say inconsiderately
rather than immorally; although many men might recognise
that – to your brother, counting the hours – your tardiness may
be an issue that merits being debated in the same breath as, say,
the morality of capital punishment.

Your brother will soon learn that to hasten your return to collect your infant, he should skip trying to make you feel guilty. Instead, he need only ask, casually, as you head for the door: 'Remind me, it's OK to splash a little gin into his bottle to help him to sleep, isn't it?'

Estate car

?   *We have two adult sons. Last year, after a stroke, their grandmother gave her car to our younger son. On her death my husband and his brother each inherited half her estate. My husband wants to share this with our sons. Should he take into account the value of the car (£1,500 to £2,000) given to the younger son, and give our elder son extra?*

It's an inheritance you're talking about, not a restaurant bill: you don't need to pore over the arithmetic to calculate who had the lobster and who ordered only a green salad.

The car given by your mother-in-law to her grandson last year was a gift she made for her own reasons. It has little to do with you. By trying to compensate now, you are undermining her gesture and her generosity. Did you spend your sons' childhood stepping in to even the score whenever you felt that aunts had bought one a nicer birthday present than the other? How do you suppose those present-givers would have felt about that? And where does such a cycle of compensation stop? If your husband gives your elder son extra to offset the car (minus depreciation, presumably), would you feel put out if your sister felt her younger nephew had now been hard done by and sent him a cheque to even things up?

Your husband should give each son an equal share, rather

than compensating for his mother's actions. It's common enough to blame your parents for messing up your life: it's trickier to start blaming them for messing up your children's lives. It's not a father's responsibility to protect his children from all life's quirky injustices. His responsibility is to make sure that, when things go wrong, his children realise that it was all their mother's fault.

Watch it!

I am thinking of buying my wife a Rolex watch to celebrate our tenth wedding anniversary. We both have biological daughters from previous marriages but no children from our own. Would it be morally OK for me to request that on her death my wife leaves the watch to my daughter from my first marriage, rather than to hers from her first marriage (my stepdaughter)?

Yes, it certainly would. Providing you didn't mind not seeing your facial features in their present familiar configuration ever again, what with your wife having slapped you so hard on hearing your request that you ended up resembling one of those Picasso portraits, with your nose sticking out from where your ear should be, and with both eyes together like a Dover sole.

What joy do you suppose your wife might reap from the watch, knowing that you see her as a temporary guardian of an item that she assumed to be a token of your love for her alone?

There is a simple rule with presents: once you make a gift of something to someone, it belongs to them. You have no further say or sway over it. If you give a gift with strings attached, it's not a gift: it's a loan for which you're retaining the title deeds as security. It's like one of those trick £5 notes you can buy from joke shops, with an invisible elastic cord attached: you hand the fiver to someone and it twangs straight back into your own pocket.

Once you have accepted the principle that a present belongs to the recipient, it is up to them what they choose to do with it. They can sell it, lose it, donate it to the church tombola, bury it in their garden, trade it in for a Patek Philippe, give it to Dan Quayle as a prize if he ever wins a spelling bee, or bequeath it to whomever they wish.

Dog's breakfast

Queuing for breakfast at a supermarket café, my two-year-old son let go of a balloon I'd passed to him, having failed to tie it. Its flight ended in a tray of bacon, which the cook then binned. Embarrassed, I sped off. Should I have coughed up for the whole tray?

You were guilty of foolishness, not malice. It was an accident. Accidents at breakfast are more forgivable than at other times, because we are at our most fragile at that time. It appalled Oscar Wilde to see that in England people try to be brilliant at breakfast when, in his eyes, 'only dull people are brilliant at breakfast'.

But the fact of something being an accident does not absolve you of all responsibility for clearing up the mess you have caused by your lack of alertness. Though you didn't mean to cost the supermarket a tray's worth of bacon, or to irritate the other queuing breakfasters, who then had to wait for a fresh batch of bacon to be frazzled, you nevertheless did.

Rather than scrambling off, you should have apologised and

offered to pay for the spoilt food. The supermarket – aware that such accidents are an unavoidable by-product of running a business in which customers are prone to make nuisances of themselves by parachuting saliva-soaked balloons into food trays, or by knocking over pyramids of Chianti bottles with wayward trolleys, or by yelping when they spot a slab of farmed salmon that's even more fluorescently orange than Robert Kilroy-Silk's complexion – would have declined your offer graciously. Your son would have been set a good example. And your digestion would have been spared the challenge of a supermarket breakfast.

Breakfast in a supermarket? What were you thinking?

Dead straight

My five-year-old son is asking me questions about the recent death of the Pope. I don't want to burden him with the idea of death at his age, so I'm skirting the issue. Is it wrong to lie to him?

Whatever you're currently telling your five-year-old about the Pope's death, the chances are it won't sound any more shocking than the tales of death he finds in storybooks.

It's only children who aren't scared by the grisly goings-on in children's books: they don't seem bothered that people die, or that the young protagonists are almost all orphans – from Harry Potter to the Baudelaire children in Lemony Snicket's successful series of novels, *A Series of Unfortunate Events*. Adults, meanwhile, find it heartbreaking that all the youths in these stories have to face life without parents, are preyed on by ogres, then have the few people they love being killed off by a villain out to seize their inheritance. Children can see fictional characters dying, or see their pets dying, without thinking immediately that this might one day happen to them. Even adults don't believe that death is about to visit any time soon, even when they do their best to taunt the Grim Reaper by smoking, or by surfing among sharks with jaws as big as a car ferry's loading bay.

Moreover, in the case of the Pope, much of the grimness traditionally associated with death is leavened by the fact that, as a Christian, he embraced the final journey to meet his maker. To a Christian, death is not a fate worse than life.

Tell your child that the Pope died peacefully, having fulfilled his work, and is now busy elsewhere. You should be honest but brief. Plant a seed in your child's mind. You needn't water it too assiduously just yet if you don't want to.

cheating on each other

? *Every day my wife does the crossword and polygon and I attempt Sudoku. I know she cheats using her electronic solver but she thinks I am unaware. I also cheat by using a computer but she does not know this. Should I mention that her cheating is known and also confess mine?*

Since the purpose of a crossword, word polygon, or Sudoku puzzle is to challenge you and, by challenging you, to make you feel quietly thrilled to have deciphered it – no, I'm sorry, that's the thrill of deciphering Donald Trump's hairdo I was thinking of.

But even with crosswords and Sudoku, many people might wonder what the point is of you and your wife cheating. Cheating at puzzles is like reaching the top of Everest by being dropped on to the peak from a helicopter. True, the view would be the same, but that's not what people climb Everest for, is it? If you and your wife are using your computer and electronic solver as aids to help you through tricky bottlenecks in puzzles, then there's nothing to feel ashamed about. It's like making your first few ascents of Everest alongside an experienced guide, absorbing from him the tricks of the trade with the aim of one day climbing the mountain under your own steam.

You know that your wife cheats, though you think she doesn't know that you know. (You might be surprised, though. Wives often know quite a lot more than you think they do. Haven't you heard of the newly married man who took an ad in a newspaper which read: 'For sale: Full set of *Encyclopaedia Britannica*. No longer needed. New wife knows everything'?) As for confronting her about her cheating? Marriage thrives on openness. But only a fool picks an argument that will benefit no one.

Gift rap

? *When my student son asked what I'd like for my birthday, I mentioned a pricey DVD set of* The Old Grey Whistle Test *TV show I nostalgically coveted. He stretched himself to buy it. But one of the discs snapped as I removed it for viewing. Do I tell him, and so hurt his feelings, or return it to a record store and pretend it was purchased there in the hope of a replacement?*

Sometimes it's not finding the right answer that's the problem, it's asking the right question. Consider these examples:

Dilemma 1: While cooking dinner for friends, poisonous drain-cleaner spills into the stewpot. Should I (a) mask the flavour by adding chillies, or (b) serve small portions to avoid killing them? Answer: Bin the food and phone for a pizza.

Dilemma 2: I see a sweater I like in a local store, only I can't afford it. Do I (a) shoplift it, or (b) get my young son to shoplift it, because if he gets caught there is less chance of the shop prosecuting? Answer: Save up and buy the sweater if I want it so badly.

Dilemma 3: I dent a stationary car while parking. Do I (a) drive away speedily so that the car-owner can't pin the blame on me, or (b) stay parked and pretend, if I'm asked, that the perpetrator was someone else? Answer: Leave an apologetic note for the absent car-owner, including contact details so that he or she can claim on my insurance.

Dilemma 4: My son pays more than he can afford to buy me a DVD I desire, but I stupidly break it. Do I (a) lie about having enjoyed it, or (b) pretend that I bought it from a local shop and claim a replacement? Answer: I go to my local store and buy a new one with my own money, thereby avoiding hurting the boy's feelings – and wallet – and getting to watch the DVD.

Getting the hang of it?

Oh brother!

? *My twin brother and I have not spoken since falling out over an inheritance five years ago. I don't want him invited to the party that my wife is throwing for my imminent retirement. My teenage son says I am being petty and has threatened to boycott the event. What should I do?*

When you say that your son thinks you're being petty, I immediately thought that at least the boy has his head screwed on tightly. But then you add that he is threatening to boycott the event, so maybe he has inherited his father's genes: you know, the ones that lead you to resolve awkwardnesses in family affairs by screwing up your eyes, jamming your fingers in your ears, then assuming that no problems exist. This is like noticing a patch of damp on a wall and – instead of calling in a specialist who will suck his teeth, slyly assess how huge a quote for repairs you're likely to swallow, then fix the problem – just covering the damp patch with plywood and a coat of paint. The result is that when you finally get around to removing the plywood years later, even a specialist glimpsing the now well-entrenched mould will emit noises like the ones Janet Leigh makes in *Psycho* when Anthony Perkins draws back the shower curtain.

Use your retirement party to start healing the rift. Whatever it is that you or your brother did, or did not, inherit, it is not important enough to overshadow, let alone crack, a bond that sounds as if it had flourished for more than half a century. Whatever was in the mind of the bequeather of the inheritance, it is unlikely that they expected their will to turn the two of you into Cain and Abel.

Of all the reasons to fall out with a sibling, money is probably the lamest. Money can't buy you happiness. Then again, happiness can't buy you money.

3 Working Models

'Anyone can do any amount of
work, provided it isn't the work
he is supposed to be doing at
that moment'

Robert Benchley

cutting a deal

In the shop where I work we are entitled to a generous staff discount on purchases for ourselves and direct family members. But a senior colleague is buying items at a discount, reselling them on eBay as new items and pocketing the profit. If not illegal, it seems immoral, and unworthy of a senior manager. Or is he doing nothing wrong?

Some people lack the discretion gauge that tells the rest of us when we have overstepped an invisible boundary. Take Pamela Anderson: having experimented with swelling her breasts to medicine-ball size and finding them a boon to her career (inasmuch as they distract audiences' attention from her acting), Anderson continued to inflate them, to the point where they are now so big that to all intents and purposes she and her nipples could be said to be living apart.

Mike Tyson didn't understand that it was wrong to bite off part of Evander Holyfield's ear, maybe reckoning that, if you're already punching someone so hard that you can make their brain bleed, then how much more barbaric can it be to chew off parts of their body?

Your discount is a small perk that, providing you're not clearing the shop out of stock, costs your boss little and makes staff happy. The store might expect that some staff might milk the perk, just as office workers might raid the stationery cupboard for the odd notebook. But by treating your shop as a wholesale supplier, your colleague is overstepping the mark. It is certainly unethical of him to exploit a staff perk to the point of setting himself up as a modest competitor. Whoever does the books will soon notice the drain on stock levels and act accordingly. Possibly by sending Mike Tyson to visit him.

Point of reference

I have been approached by a dear friend of ten years' standing for a reference for a new job. It involves working in some elderly people's homes. My friend is a hard-working, caring person but, alas, has 'magpie' tendencies. Among the items that she purloins are restaurant napkins and cutlery. How should this reference be worded?

Saying that your friend is hard-working but, alas, has magpie tendencies is like saying that Dick Cheney is a hard-working US Vice-President who, alas, has a tendency to shoot his friends while out quail-hunting; or that Noel Edmonds is a successful TV presenter who, alas, has a tendency to make you feel queasy whenever he appears on screen; or that Michael Jackson sings catchy tunes but, alas, has a tendency to dangle his children over balconies.

In terms of truthfulness and accuracy, the CVs and references of many job applicants are right up there with that infamous intelligence dossier on Iraq. Nevertheless, there is quite a difference between someone burnishing the pass grade for their Media Studies GCSE and inventing the possession of a wholly fictitious medical degree ('Don't worry about a thing, Mrs Brimple. The operation's going to go just fine because – see here? – I'm using my rabbit's-foot-handle scalpel!').

Your friend's case falls between these two extremes. But would you sleep easily if, as a result of your reference, your friend landed a job that allowed her to indulge her 'magpie' tendencies in your grandmother's house? No? Then you cannot avoid mentioning her thievery. Alternatively, recommend her for a job in one of those motorway service-station cafés that make you eat with plastic cutlery and paper napkins, where her magpie tendencies will be thwarted.

Attractive prospect

A would-be client has become very flirtatious. I'm pretty certain his attraction is genuine and would exist regardless of the business context, but I am worried he's doing it just to get the work. Is it wrong to continue down this path before the decision is made about who gets the job? I am confident that I can separate the two issues in my head.

How does this would-be client flirt with you? Does he say 'Look, I don't care whether I land the business or not, I'd just like to see more of you'? Or does he say 'Would you like to spend the weekend at the Ritz in Paris, making love like Donald Sutherland and Julie Christie in *Don't Look Now*, only without anyone even having to pay us millions of dollars first? Have I got the new contract? Could you answer the second question first?'

Try testing his ardour (he does have an ardour, I take it?

Otherwise you should both seek medical guidance before taking the relationship any further) with a white lie: tell him that, while the decision hasn't been officially announced, you happen to know that he hasn't got the work, and see if he still shows any interest in flirting with you when there's no commercial windfall in it for him.

If this suitor still wants to take you to dinner, then his flirting may be genuine. But if his vision of your life together suddenly starts veering towards Groucho Marx's wooing of Margaret Dumont – 'Married! I can see you now, in the kitchen, bending over a hot stove, but I can't see the stove' – then chances are he'll start discreetly distancing himself from you.

Oh, and you can separate the two issues in your head, can you? Look, if people could keep a straight head while whoozy with urgent sexual desire, then David Gest would still be a virgin.

Bet noire

> **?** *My managing director called from his conference asking me to put £10 to win on a 15-1 outsider running at York. I forgot. Fortunately, the horse didn't even place. Should I now say 'Unlucky, boss, but you owe me a tenner' or reveal that I forgot to place the bet?*

A tricky one, morally speaking. If you are not a bookmaker, you have no right to take the tenner from your boss, and to then just count yourself lucky that you were spared having to stump up £150 had his horse come in first. You just happened to be lucky that your boss chose a weak horse: or, to put it a kinder way, that he chose a horse that was so good that it took several others to beat it.

Actually, you were not lucky, exactly, since if you were to compare the net gains made by non-gamblers from not betting (namely, nothing) against the net returns secured by gamblers as a result of a lifetime of betting, you'd find that 'luck' tended to favour the non-gamblers.

The complication in your case is that, had you failed to place this bet on behalf of, say, a friend, that friend's irritation at your unreliability may have been eclipsed by relief at having ended up £10 richer than they might otherwise have done. But your boss's gratitude at being spared a £10 loss may well be overshadowed by his concerns over your unreliability. It may not be the most noble way to behave, but you might just avoid mentioning the bet ever again in the hope that your boss forgets about it, too. If he insists on paying up, make a show of placing the tenner on another horse, and splitting the booty with him if it wins.

Watch case

? *As a partnership, we bought our retiring senior partner an expensive watch. Our budget was £1,000. We eventually spent £1,250 for a watch which we thought would be particularly appreciated. Sadly the receiver asked for the watch to be returned and requested the money instead. Should we pay him the whole amount, or just the £1,000 which was the sum we had first intended to spend?*

Maybe your retiring senior partner was not so much ungrateful for your generous gift as he was confused as to why on the occasion of his retirement – perhaps the first time in a professional career of four or five decades that he no longer has to monitor the clock to ensure that he makes the 07.19 into

Waterloo, or to bill his clients by the hour – his colleagues thought that what he might now need most in life is an expensive wristwatch. ('It's 11.17 a.m. . . . Oh look, it's now 11.23 a.m. My retirement is whizzing away.') It's also possible that the watch you gave him just wasn't high-tech enough. Judging by the advertisements, the majority of wristwatches are now the size of a teacake, on account of incorporating stopwatch facilities, depth and altitude gauges, miniature George Foreman grills and such like. Should the wearer ever need to check his height above sea level on the way to the office, then – bingo! – all the chronometry he needs is right there on his wrist.

Your senior partner didn't know how much you had intended to spend. He only knows how much you did spend – by checking the watch's list price. Increasing your gift to £1,250 was a measure of the depth of your admiration for your colleague; otherwise you would have stuck to your original budget. It would be mean-spirited, hurtful and unethical to backtrack now.

Law of supply and demand

Fellow students offered to buy study notes I have compiled for my law degree. I refused because degrees are awarded on aggregate scores, so helping others might hurt my chances of landing a top grade. But would it be unethical to sell my notes to next year's crop of aspiring lawyers, given that, as a barrister, I plan to make my living from selling my academic knowledge?

As you are evidently learning, law is the surest way to make crime pay. The ideal client for a lawyer is, famously, someone who has plenty of money and is in deep trouble; which sounds pretty much a description of your fellow undergraduates. And since you have a talent for shaping your scruples to fit the brief (providing the fee is large enough), you may possess the ideal credentials to become a successful lawyer. But also an ethical one?

It's true that you'll be making a career from selling your knowledge of the law. But that doesn't mean that representing clients in a courtroom and selling your university law notes to lazy students are just alternative ways of skinning the same cat – little different, say, from a butcher selling steak to a fireman, on the one hand, and to a nurse, on the other. In fact, it's more like the difference between offering morphine to someone in pain and selling it to a junkie.

Of course, having just completed a law degree, you may not be able to help blurring the boundary between what is lawful and what is right, since a key aim of a first-class training in jurisprudence is mastering how to convince a jury on a point of law, not on a point of justice. Unless, of course, the lawyer is Perry Mason, who was not only always right but also won all his cases inside an hour, including commercial breaks. Why don't students buy his law notes instead?

Bare-faced cheek

?   *After my lodger, who is also a friend and work colleague, moved out, I discovered a DVD entitled* Real Girls Striptease *under his mattress. It shocks me that he should own a DVD so degrading to women, and I am wondering how best to return it to him. Would it be unethical to leave it on his desk at work, where colleagues may see it, causing him embarrassment?*

It's always a shock, isn't it, to discover things about people you thought you knew well? I mean, who'd have guessed, merely from having watched *The Passion of The Christ*, that Mel Gibson was the sort of person who'd believe that Jews were responsible for everything that's wrong in the world, from wars to elephant-poaching? (You need a very big casserole to do this.) *Real Girls Striptease* may not be the sort of DVD that many of us would want to watch (and I'm using 'many of us' here in its sense of 'most women'), but it doesn't sound as if it is an illegal porn video. It may sadden you, repulse you even, that such DVDs are on general sale: that is understandable. But to make an end-user bear the entire burden of blame? That seems as unfair as Interpol making an example of a casual pot-smoker in Widnes, while making no effort also to bring to justice the crime syndicates that run the drugs trade.

As for leaving the DVD on your ex-lodger's office desk? Ha, ha, ha! Far from embarrassing him, this will almost certainly result in the DVD being 'borrowed' by a colleague before your friend even arrives for work, denying him even the possibility of feeling ashamed. That's how many offices seem to work. You could leave a DVD of *Donald Trump's Home Hairstyling Tips* and someone would still 'borrow' it, just in case they might ever think of a use for it one day.

Taxing wait

Though I gave my accountant all my tax papers last May, he filed my return mere days before the January 31 deadline. For months I was unable to speak to him, his assistant telling me that he was 'downstairs', or 'seeing a client'. He'd actually had several strokes. I'd feel mean removing my business now, yet I resent paying for an accountant who tells lies to his clients. What should I do?

Hello? Hello? Yoo-hoo! Anyone out there still reading this? I know that most of you will have stopped reading and be in a state of shock after the bit where it says, 'though I gave my accountant all my tax papers last May'; much the way in which Charles Darwin might have been stopped in his tracks, while visiting the Galapagos, by the sight of a hitherto unknown species.

Who hands over tax papers to their accountant in May, for Pete's sake? Accountants don't know what to do with tax paperwork in May. They are like journalists. They work best as a deadline approaches – although obviously, unlike journalists, accountants don't feel tempted to invent a few handily supportive quotes as that deadline looms ('Dear Tax Inspector, while there may be no actual invoices or receipts to corroborate the outgoings listed on page four of my client's return, several well-placed sources, who requested anonymity, have vouched for their authenticity').

Compassion might steer you towards maintaining your relationship with your accountant. You might reasonably ask that, in return for your loyalty, he should be honest with you, were his health to disrupt his work again. As for your resenting paying for an accountant who lies to his clients, you're right. We pay accountants to lie to the taxman.

Talk isn't cheap

I employ seven Pakistanis (legally, with work permits and visas). I have hired a tutor to improve their English. I meet this cost myself because if their English improves it will benefit me. But may I not pass on the cost to them because, in the long run, better English will probably boost their job prospects, if and when they leave my employment?

Would you arrange sewing lessons for them and then deduct the cost from their wages on the ground that learning how to handle a needle and thread will save them a fortune in clothes repairs, and even more if they become adept enough to run up some of their own shirts? You wouldn't? Then why deduct the expenses of their English lessons without first consulting them?

Being abroad and not being able to converse with the natives in their tongue is always a nuisance; as Dan Quayle found when, during a trip as US Vice-President, he apologised for not being able to 'address the people of Latin America in their own language, Latin'. You acknowledge that you will benefit from your workers' improved fluency in English; and they may well be grateful enough for the free lessons to repay you with loyalty. Companies don't charge employees when they send them on training courses to acquire skills that benefit the company, even though these skills might also enhance the employees' future job prospects.

You may find that even without formal tutoring, your Pakistani employees pick up certain key phrases they find they need to get by in their new homeland: such as, 'What are these deductions from our wages for English lessons? Is it a tax for people who can't speak English in a comprehensible manner? If so, is it deducted from George Bush's wages, too?'

Odds and ends

A work colleague has been treated unfairly, having been denied a pay rise after a year of hard work. She is on a much lower salary than the rest of us and decided to resign. Another colleague and I decided to place a bet on whether she would or would not resign the next day. Is it morally wrong to place such bets?

My hunch is that it would certainly seem to be immoral to make money from another's misfortunes by betting on whether a shoddily-treated colleague will have the guts to resign. But it might also be tricky to see how most gambling doesn't, then, come down to betting on another's misfortunes, at least in some way. Take poker, for instance: if you win the pot, then someone else has lost it. On the racetrack, if your horse wins, another punter's doesn't.

This equation holds even in the more camouflaged forms of gambling, to which we give fancy names so as to hide the fact that they are, in many ways, little different from casinos. Forms such as stock markets: if you buy shares because you expect their value to rise, the sucker who sold them to you has lost out on some profit. Equally, if you buy shares expecting them to go up and their price plummets, whoever sold them is cashing in on your loss.

In this sense, betting on whether or not someone is about to make themselves jobless might be seen as little different from betting on when an earthquake might next strike San Francisco; or whether it will rain throughout the first week of Wimbledon, ruining a treat for thousands of Centre Court ticket-holders; or whether James Blunt will be stricken by laryngitis when next entering a recording studio. The book that you and your colleague opened was in bad taste, but not necessarily immoral.

Free advice

Though the store where I work is running a buy-one, get-one-free offer that is promoted via highly visible posters and signs, not all customers notice them, and they come to the counter with just one item. My boss says that I should keep quiet because it's their fault for not reading the sign. I feel that the customer should be told; but, then, it's not my money invested in the business ...

There is every chance that some customers are aware of the shop's promotion but just happen not to need two of whatever they are buying. They think it is more sound, environmentally, even if financially less advantageous, to decline the offer of a duplicate product.

Then again, you never know how some people will behave if offered something free. I was at a superstore two days before Christmas when shoppers waiting to pay for their Christmas trees were told that the store was no longer charging for the few trees it had left. Some shoppers just thanked the store and their good fortune. Others carried their tree to their car and immediately went back for more. Where did they put them all? (BILLY: 'You've certainly got plenty of Christmas trees in your sitting room this year, Walter.' WALTER: 'We're going for a Black Forest theme. There are more pines in the bedrooms upstairs. And a few trees on the roof. If the supermarket had had Sachertorte on buy-one, get-one-free, our Christmas would be made. Made, I tell you!') But this is a shopper's decision to make. If your boss does not want customers to take up the offer, why make it? Its purpose is to entice shoppers and win their loyalty. If they don't even notice, the promotion is failing. You are right to alert shoppers to the offer. It is their right to spurn it.

Jobs for the girls

I have been encouraging a woman who works in a company on the floor above to look for a new job. A move would do her good, and because I don't much like her, it would also save me having to talk to her. While seeking my view on vacancies, she showed me one, which sounds great – but for me, not her. Is it wrong for me to phone the agency on my own behalf?

Not especially, I suppose, since you could even have spotted the advertisement yourself – if you weren't so otherwise occupied scheming to reconfigure your work environment. But listen, have you considered the possibility that, far from being the dullard you take her for, your upstairs neighbour may simply have tired of you as much as you have of her? And that rather than quit a job she enjoys just so that she might be spared the sight of you in the lift every day, she is deliberately dangling before your eyes this bait of job vacancies that she knows might tempt you?

The blind spot of many Machiavellian-minded people is that they rarely credit the possibility that their targets might be as Machiavellian as they are. People flattered to be phoned by headhunters might be less flattered if they knew how often it was their boss who had sung their praises to the headhunter in the hope of easing them off the payroll without tears (or a payoff).

So how will you be able to tell whether you've been outmanoeuvred? By noting who's celebrating most when you land that job to which she alerted you: you or Miss Dullard from upstairs. Kierkegaard said that the great trick with a woman is to get rid of her while she thinks she's getting rid of you. OK, so he probably didn't have quite this situation in mind; but it applies all the same.

classy whine

My husband, a member of the school parent-teacher association, ordered several cases of wine from a supermarket for a school event. They delivered one case too many. He was intending to drink to his luck, until I persuaded him to alert the supermarket, which said it would arrange collection the following day. Three weeks have passed. Can we now drink the wine without guilt?

Yes, wouldn't that be great if guilt had a sell-by date attached? You could set the kitchen timer, wait for it to ping and – bingo! – the time for any guilt would have expired.

The guilt you may feel is not the same guilt to which judges refer when passing sentence. That kind of guilt does carry an expiry date, a time by which a criminal is deemed to have repaid his debt to society. This expiry date can even be brought forward for good behaviour (waiting for three weeks before uncorking your windfall wine does not count as good behaviour).

It's not as if you even paid for the wine: the extra case belongs to the supermarket. If you wished to play God and penalise the store for its incompetence, then the windfall should go to the school (and, Lord knows, any school event involving parents and teachers could do with an extra case of wine in circulation) that footed the bill for the consignment; not to your husband, who was merely the middleman. Your husband is a member of the school's parent-teacher association, not a wine broker, slicing off an intermediary's margin on every transaction.

You can drink the wine without chilling it; or without bringing it to room temperature. You can drink the wine without company to share it. You can drink it without decanting it. You can drink it without cheese; or without fanfare. You just can't drink it without guilt.

Tip-off

? *If a tradesperson who usually works independently finds himself working with another tradesperson while refurbishing a client's house, is it in order for the last man off the site to keep the client's tip, or should he share it with the other tradesperson?*

You must share any tip given by the client with the other tradesperson with whom you are working (although by that stage in a building project the tip the client most usually wants to give to contractors is: 'Why don't you consider learning the basics of plumbing before you next install a bathroom?'). You must share it, not just because it is morally the right course, but because otherwise on the last day of a job, the client would be forced to play host late into the night to a swarm of tradespeople, each of whom was determined to outstay the others until he was left as the last person on site and thus able to scoop the entire tip for himself.

If anything, handing the tip to the first tradesman on site seems smarter. Where is the sense in tipping someone after they've provided a service, when it's too late to affect anything? A tip is a bribe to someone to treat you well, so it should be given in advance. If you tipped a bellboy as soon as he opened your hotel room door, you'd have an extra ten minutes of holiday because he wouldn't then bother hanging around to explain how to operate the TV, or the concept of a bed ('You pull back the sheets, like so; lie down for a few hours, then get up again').

Muggers have rumbled the right priority, making it a policy to ask you for a tip in advance if you want to be spared from being stabbed. Given the quality of some tradespeople's work, that may be the most apt example to follow.

Wild bore

I have a colleague at work who, while professional and civil, is boring. Whenever I bump into him on my way to the railway station after work I'm stumped for things to say. Should I buy a car?

A colleague who is professional and civil, but boring, may not be the person with whom you most want to make small talk on your journey home from work, this being a time when you might prefer the sort of solitude that allows you to focus intently on how best to get even with various other colleagues who are more diverting, but also unprofessional and rude.

To avoid your boring colleague, consider taking up a teach-yourself-Spanish course that requires you to listen to educational CDs on the train to and from work. When you next bump into your workmate, after a few initial pleasantries you'll be able to produce your CD earphones, shrug apologetically, and explain that you must press on because you're visiting Madrid/taking a GCSE in Spanish/need to reach the section that covers domestic matters so that you can explain to your new Spanish-only-speaking cleaner that Marmite is a food product, not a furniture polish. This solves your problem and carries an educational bonus.

Or you could use your colleague's boringness to your advantage, the way a sumo wrestler exploits an opponent's weight by sending him tumbling when he's off-balance: you yourself must develop a line in commuter conversation so dull that it is your colleague who is eager to find a different carriage whenever he spots you on the platform.

By the way, ever wondered whether your colleague already finds you so boring that his heart, too, sinks when he spots you on the station platform, but is himself too civil to desert you?

Double take

A company offered me a job last week, pending reference checks. But I have since been interviewed for a job which appeals to me more. Is it unethical to accept the first job when the formal offer arrives, knowing that I will probably take the second position if it is offered to me? Or should I warn the first company to look for someone else, just in case?

Or maybe you should just short-circuit the whole process and tell the first employer: 'Just sack me now.'

Unless you're Leonardo DiCaprio, and unless the first employer is a film studio that is happy to wait while you choose between a movie in which they want to cast you and an alternative movie proposal from a rival Hollywood studio, then the chances are that this employer will not be thrilled to hear that it has wasted its time interviewing you and checking your references only for you to reveal belatedly that, actually, your heart lies elsewhere. It's like hearing a woman tell you: 'Sure I'll go on a date with you on Saturday. But only if I can't scrape up a more enticing offer by the weekend – oh, and by "more enticing" I mean "including an entire evening spent with David Gest without my even wearing a blindfold".'

The tricky part is that this is one of those areas where ethics and self-interest intersect at such an inconvenient angle that most people find it easiest to pretend that the graph doesn't exist. Who could blame them? With no guarantee that the second employer will pick you for its vacancy, few would gamble on rejecting the offer from the first company. Fewer still would be so ethically honourable as to inform the first employer that they'll be accepting the job being offered – but only after another company has deemed them to be not worth employing.

Profits all round

A leaving collection for a work colleague produced just enough to buy the silver vase the leaver had asked for. But when I went to buy it, the shop had a sale, so I saved 5 per cent on the regular price. Can I pocket the profit on the basis that the leaver got the present that he wanted, and I got something for my trouble in organising the collection and buying the vase?

It's not so much your departing work colleague who would be out of pocket as a result of your proposal, but those people who will remain your work colleagues. The leaver may be getting the vase he wished for, but those who chipped in to pay for it might reasonably expect that all the cash they donated to the leaving fund was lavished on its recipient. You volunteered yourself as a collection-organiser, not a wholesaler with a licence to scalp a profit if he could broker a margin between income and outgoings.

What are you, some kind of corporate gift tout? Do you loiter outside office leaving parties, waving vases and wristwatches and hissing: 'Presents! Who wants presents for tonight's leaving do? I'm buying, too: who's got leaving presents they want to sell?' Tell me, if a stranger collapsed on the pavement and, like a good citizen, you drove him to a hospital, would you bill the ambulance service for the money it had saved as a result of your kind action, what with your having spared it from having to come to the invalid's aid?

You're evidently one of those people who believes that if something's worth doing, it's worth doing for money. Want to know whether keeping the 5 per cent is acceptable? Then ask yourself: would you be happy for your colleagues to find out that they'd lined your pockets?

Plumb Line

My son had a summer job at a plumbers' merchant, where sales staff were given discretion to offer customers a 10 per cent discount. Fellow sales staff gave it, if asked, to regular or large-order customers. Our son awarded it depending on how polite or rude a plumber was. His system made the most profit for the company. Was he being ethical?

What is most amazing about overhearing plumbers buying supplies is how knowledgeable they sound, compared with how they sound when they visit your house.

On home visits, plumbers divide into those who refer to every key component of a central heating system, or of a shower unit, as a 'wossname', and those who converse in obscure technical jargon ('It's your oscillating confibulatory valve that's compressing the inlet upshaft's transregulator') to gauge how easily you scare, meanwhile furtively adding more zeros to their estimate the more haunted you look.

It's not entirely clear, from the information you provide, how exactly your son came to notch up the most profit for his company. Was it because the plumbers were generally so rude that he found very little occasion to grant them his discretionary 10 per cent discount, thereby resulting in his taking almost 10 per cent more than some of his fellow salesmen?

Let's be generous, though, and assume that your son's criterion for granting a discount – namely, a plumber's politeness – was the engine which generated his extra sales, resulting in extra profits. Was he being ethical? Yes, in the utilitarian sense that he managed to achieve the greatest good for the greatest number: a courteous working environment, and swollen profits for his bosses. Virtue is its own reward; but it also, in this case, brought its own rewards.

Tennis racket

> **?** *I have won two tickets to the Wimbledon men's final in a competition open to all employees in my company. The competition involved skilfully putting my name on a coupon. These tickets would buy a nice family holiday. I'm in no doubt that flogging them is against the spirit of the competition, but others are adamant that I am entitled to do whatever I like with the tickets.*

You don't have a moral obligation to keep everything that you win in a competition. If everyone kept everything they'd won from vicarage fête tombola stalls over the course of their lives, then the shelves of charity shops would be bare and eBay would be out of business.

And then where would we be? If you suddenly decided that you could no longer live without owning a novelty corkscrew in the shape of a raven-haired female flamenco dancer whose legs rise sideways in an anatomically alarming manner as the coiled screw winds deeper and deeper into the wine cork, then you'd have to fly all the way to Alicante to buy one for yourself.

Had you won the tickets in an anonymous pub raffle, you might have fewer qualms about flogging them. Just because you won them at the office doesn't alter the principle. If an aunt sacrifices her own Glyndebourne tickets because she knows that you love *The Magic Flute*, she might have cause to feel aggrieved if you sold them to a tout. The prize in an office sweepstake is not freighted with the same emotional or ethical baggage.

Of course, it could be that your tickets are two of four Centre Court debentures owned by your company's chairman, who'll be expecting to meet his lucky employee on Finals Day. What if you sell your tickets to a stranger who gets frisky with the boss's spouse? Tricky career move, that.

Testing dilemma

My son got a B grade for his GCSE English coursework. He's sometimes a bit haphazard on grammar and punctuation: had he allowed me to read through it and suggest changes, he might have got an A. Would this have been cheating, or merely using the opportunity to teach him something he hasn't picked up at school? I'm sure many parents do help with coursework.

I've heard of children attending the swankiest schools whose novelist parents type out their offspring's English coursework for them. And sons of doctors who get their parents to cast an eye over (that is, to rewrite) their science coursework. (One danger, of course, is that your son's maths coursework gets sent home with a note from the teacher saying: 'Dear Jack, Please tell your dad that we don't prove Pythagoras this way any more.') There is no intrinsic virtue in leaving a pupil in the dark when he could be enlightened by being directed to a book, a fact, a poem or a learned essay that might help him to do a better job of his homework and thereby advance his education. But nor is there any obvious virtue in garlanding a child with unearned A grades that give him a false sense of his own talents.

Is it ethical to 'revise' your son's school work? No, it isn't. Is it ethical to let him fare comparatively worse than his classmates because they've been helped by their parents? That doesn't sound fair either, does it? But grades have always been a fool's yardstick. Your son has done well without your help. He may even benefit from making his own mistakes and relishing his own successes.

In the meantime, maybe there should be a new marking system. We could call it an A grade (PA), to denote 'Parent-Assisted', and it could be equivalent to a B grade (Non-PA).

Learning to share

With our GCSEs approaching, a friend and I went to a revision class at a school across the city. On showing our teacher a booklet containing helpful revision advice that we'd been given, she asked whether she could study it. If she were to photocopy it and hand it out to the rest of the class, should I feel cheated, as we were the ones who put in the time and effort to go?

Even in education, it seems, the tastiest-looking fruit always hangs on someone else's tree. Will Rogers suggested exploiting this avaricious itch that people suddenly develop to get their hands on something the minute they feel they're being denied it. How? Rogers floated the idea of treating education in the same way that liquor was treated during Prohibition. He suggested banning everyone from learning anything, and reckoned that if the system worked even half as well as Prohibition, America within five years would have the smartest people on Earth.

It is one of the tragedies of the British education system that even children now regard exam results as the sole barometer of educational progress, occasionally to the point of thinking that scoring top grades is not good enough: for that success to taste truly sweet, it is also important that their schoolmates fare worse.

Why? Education is like manure: the more broadly it is spread, the more good it does. If it's concentrated in one person, you end up with Wittgenstein, who was ferociously smart, but was always wondering about suicide. It doesn't make you any less bright that both you and I know that the Treaty of Versailles was signed in 1919. And Latin is always useful. Remember: all education contributes to the *summum bonum* (literally, 'helps you earn a fatter salary').

Moral Vacuum

My lovely, trusty Estonian gem of a cleaner accidentally broke my two-month-old cylinder cleaner last week by, I assume, inadvertently letting it fall down the stairs. It cost £149 and she is off on her second holiday abroad this month. What is the right thing to do?

As a general rule, breakages by cleaners are footed either by the houseowner or, if the replacement cost is high, by an insurance claim – unless, of course, the general making the general rule is Franco, in which case the cleaner would probably just be put before a firing squad.

It's true that there's no reason why workplaces shouldn't follow the same rules as those shops that attach twee tags to trinkets reading 'If you break me, you own me'; which instantly encourage you to find a mallet with which to hit the tagged object very hard. Wait! I remember why: because if we had to pay for workplace breakages, nobody would take home a salary after deductions for damages had been made. People do reckless things to their office computer which, if they saw their child doing the same on their home PC, would make an adult's hair stand out like a porcupine's quills. But confronted by a recalcitrant office computer, people will happily keep jabbing keys. Why? Because they know that, if all else fails, they can just call the folk in the IT department, who – within just two minutes of hearing the symptoms – always manage to tell them: 'We'll have to wipe the hard disk and rebuild it from scratch.'

Maybe the cleaner (cylinder, not Estonian) is just faulty. Unless your gem is making a habit of breaking your cleaners, it seems harsh to bill her. Then again, if she *is* making a habit of it, get her a job in a lab where they test the resilience of household appliances to punishing everyday use.

All going swimmingly

I've decided not to finish my university course, and to drop out. However, I've been thinking of buying a year's pass to the university swimming pool, though haven't got around to it. Would it be unethical to buy such a pass now, while I am still a student, and thus at the student rate, and use it during the year after I've left?

Anyone so keen on swimming that they would actually see a worthwhile return from buying an annual pool pass may well be taking swimming too seriously. Freud believed that swimming disguised a yearning to return to the amniotic waters of the womb; which, given the average university pool, suggests that wombs are full of over-chlorinated, verruca-infested water and detached sticking plasters. Or maybe Viennese women are just built differently.

Swinburne enjoyed swimming because the 'lash and sting' of the sea's surf evoked erotic memories of the floggings he received as a schoolboy at Eton, while Flaubert likened the sensation of swimming to 'a thousand liquid nipples travelling over the body'. Byron, who swam daily at a stagnant duck-pond near Newstead Abbey, took to water with such relish that, on leaving a party in Venice, he dived fully clothed into the Grand Canal and swam home. You start to wonder whether university-level intellect and swimming are a healthy combination, don't you?

Had you bought the swimming pass while still happy in your studies, then enjoying use of the pool after having decided to leave would have been an accidental by-product. Choosing to buy a pass now might seem to produce the same end result, but leaves you in trickier ethical waters. Since you are half in the wrong, maybe you should get into the pool only up to your waist.

copy right?

? *Our department at the school where I teach was close to overspending its photocopying budget. Our head of department stopped our photocopying code, but a colleague gave me an admin code to use. Should I feel guilty about using it?*

It may be hard for some people who went to school decades ago to appreciate just how key a role photocopies play in modern learning. What with schools unable to afford enough textbooks for their pupils, many teachers rely on handing them photocopies of information.

The alternative for teachers is to ask pupils to conduct their own research at home using modern technology. This amounts to (a) scavenging a few facts from the *You Say, We Pay* segment on the *Richard and Judy* TV show; (b) learning from TV commercials about hitherto unknown chemicals that lend glossiness to even the dullest hair; or else (c) using Google, which explains why so many pupils' history homework reveals that Marco Polo was a famous Venetian airport with several direct flights a day from Heathrow, and an idyllic gateway for a romantic weekend.

Photocopies are now often the surest way teachers have for channelling information from authoritative sources for their pupils to copy out at home and pass off as the fruits of their own intelligence; which actually happens to be an almost perfect preparation for journalism. So think of bending the rules on photocopying budgets not as moral weakness, more a moral duty.

Sick Leave

I have accepted annual leave from the NHS over Christmas. Is it now immoral for me to locum over this period for a company that offers to pay me obscene amounts of money? I am anxious about NHS colleagues finding out that I have exploited this mercenary opportunity. I am single and have no immediate family with whom to spend Christmas. Does this absolve me of any guilt?

You may be doing nothing illegal by freelancing as a locum during your Christmas break (unless, of course, your NHS contract forbids you from working for others). But the fact that you nevertheless feel twitchy about how your NHS colleagues might react if they were to learn of your lucrative off-duty employment suggests that you sense a moral muddiness to your position.

Actually, it's more of a paradoxical muddiness. How is it that a private company can offer you such generously paid work as a locum over the Christmas period? Because many NHS employees do not wish to work over the holidays; and since just as many people get sick at Christmas, this creates an imbalance between the demand for, and supply of, doctors and nurses.

But here's the paradox: if you didn't take annual leave from your NHS post at Christmas, then there wouldn't be the shortage of NHS staff that generates the vacuum for locums to fill. In other words, far from simply seizing a serendipitous opportunity that happens to have come your way, you have helped to engineer that opportunity in the first place by removing yourself from NHS Christmas rotas. What's more, the longer the holidays you take, the greater the amount of lucrative work you will generate for yourself in the private sector. Brilliant, eh?

Way over the top

? *At my boarding school it is not unusual for stuff to go 'missing'. A friend's favourite top disappeared, only to turn up in another girl's bedroom. Being sure it was hers, we decided to take it back. The girl has not made any comment about having had a top stolen, whereas usually it's a big thing and the whole year gets involved. Were we right to take the top back?*

You may probably realise this already, but much of what you are learning in the classroom today will prove to be of very little obvious use in the decades ahead.

Fractions? They don't exist in the real world. Nor is there much chance that you will ever need to work out the area of a semicircle. Knowing how to calculate the hypotenuse of a triangle impresses nobody after you've satisfied your maths GCSE examiner. And as for the number of times you're going to need to know the annual rainfall in Caracas, you might as well just live dangerously when visiting Venezuela and buy an umbrella if you're caught out in an unexpected downpour.

A school's far more important role is to prepare you for real life, including learning the art of rubbing along with other people, the art of diplomacy, and the art of getting even. In short, you must make sure that you never let your schooling stand in the way of your education. Greed, jealousy, theft, deceit – these are things you will encounter in life more often than you will logarithms or copper sulphate. If you're going to steal back clothes as an experiment to see how fellow members of society react, then boarding school may be the place to get it out of your system. But if you've reached the stage where you're writing essays entitled, *What I'm Going to Steal When I Grow Up*, then you've probably gone a little too far.

Grape Shot

? *At a wine-tasting with a client's staff, their MD interrupted our sales lady to explain that any wine with two parts to its name was made from two grape varieties – sauvignon blanc, for example, being 60 per cent sauvignon and 40 per cent blanc. Rather than correct, and humiliate, him in front of his staff, our sales lady let it pass. Did she do the right thing?*

It is always awkward when someone uses a foreign word or phrase in a way that betrays that he doesn't understand its meaning, an embarrassing situation which would have led Ancient Romans to sigh, wisely, *Errare humanum est* (Latin for 'He's a real weirdo!').

This kind of slip-up shows that when it comes to using foreign words in his conversation, the man is clearly not *au courant* (literally, 'running water') and needs a linguistic wake-up call (*tout a l'heure*). But since the mistake was probably an innocent one, the best way for your sales lady to avoid a scene would be to treat him sympathetically by greeting him a *bras ouverts* ('wearing provocative lingerie'). Have I made myself clear?

Your sales lady did the right thing. Humiliating the boss in front of his staff would have achieved little and potentially damaged much – far beyond your company's contract for further wine-tastings. Had the MD been pontificating erroneously about which button not to press to avoid launching a nuclear missile, then it would certainly have been wisest to put him right. His staff probably knew he was talking tosh, anyway. It may be that the MD's apparent faux pas was actually deliberate, and you were being secretly filmed for a TV prank show. The key thing to remember in such linguistic situations is never to resort to *ipsissima verba* (rude language).

Keeping good time

I employ two girls to work from 10 a.m. to noon daily. They note in a book when they arrive and depart because I pay them by the hour. Lately, both have been arriving at around 10.20 and leaving just before midday. But the book says 10 a.m. to noon. I have been paying them for the hours the book says, but I am becoming bothered by their fibs.

Though you are in a distressing situation, it would be wrong to draw the conclusion from your particular and minor case that all young casual workers come in late for their shift and leave early. Some don't bother coming in at all.

Many employed people wear two watches. They wear their 'work watch', which often runs up to half an hour late: this means they arrive at the office just as their more diligent colleagues are busily rushing off for their important two-hour mid-morning coffee break. Then they have their 'leisure watch', which runs twenty minutes fast so that they can be sure of getting to the cinema in time to grab two good seats, one for them and one for a bucket of popcorn large enough to feed the entire cast of the movie they are about to watch.

You must decide whether your two girls accomplish more in the hour and a half that they actually do work than they might if serving their full two hours under sufferance. You don't mention if the problem is work being left undone (which is easily enough remedied by ensuring that they do all that is needed before they bunk off) or whether you just don't like being taken for a ride.

Clocks are, anyway, not always the most reliable way to measure a person's output. I'd rather have Henri Matisse painting for a day than Tracey Emin painting for a month. Wouldn't you?

File under 'No'

? *I'm a hard-working student who keeps his work in a neat filing system. Unfortunately, when my back is turned, two acquaintances of mine find it highly amusing to bend my folder as a 'joke'. Does that give me moral entitlement to bend theirs?*

It gives you a moral entitlement to be irritated, but if you find their behaviour puerile, why would you then want to imitate it? That would be like the Prince of Wales saying nasty things about the press just because the press says nasty things about him – hang on, he *does* say nasty things about the press. And have you noticed how much good it does him?

Anyway, as a general rule, it's never a smart idea to respond instinctively, like fat in a fire, when somebody annoys you. Counting to ten first will calm you down, and allow you time to devise a spikier response than you could have dreamt up on the spur of the moment. But what response? No need to go over-board. When he was in power in Russia, Khrushchev recalled in his memoirs: 'We had no use for the policy of the Gospels: if someone slaps you, just turn the other cheek. We had shown that anyone who slapped us on our cheek,' he boasted proudly, 'would get his head kicked off.' But I'm pretty sure that Khrushchev was talking about something more troublesome than an upstart neighbour bending a folder as a joke.

The bending over of folders is not a subject that has troubled many moral philosophers although, as a rule, they divide between the turn-the-other-cheek brigade and the eye-for-an-eye faction. It's commendable that you're happy to limit your planned vengeance to a proportionate response, but folder-bending seems too petty a tit to merit even a reciprocal tat.

Gambling on a new career

I have been offered a good job with an online marketing company which, I have now found out, handles business for gambling sites. I am strongly opposed to gambling, having met many people whose lives have been blighted by it. Can I refuse to handle business for gaming clients?

The one thing that gamblers have going for them is their optimism. Even after a big loss, they remain confident that the next horse they back will not again be so slow that it gets overtaken by that fellow who follows each race with a bucket, shovelling up the horse poop.

What gamblers have going against them is also their optimism, which spurs them on to place bets when fully sober that most people wouldn't make even after a bottle of absinthe. Gambling, at its worse, can prove to be not just a waste of money, but a waste of life. So your concerns about helping a gaming site to lure more punters may be understandable enough.

But if you have such a strong moral aversion to gambling that you prefer not to involve yourself in the part of your company's business that deals with online gaming sites, would it not be unethical to draw a salary from an organisation whose profits are at least partly swollen by income it receives from servicing these same gaming-site clients? Wouldn't that be like a vegan agreeing to work in a farm shop providing he was allowed to sell only vegetables and was never asked to serve customers wanting a shoulder of lamb or a piece of veal?

It can become tricky if you want to pick and choose how to splice your ethics. If you are a woman and you – quite understandably – bridle at men ogling you on a train, you can't then blush and swoon if the man doing the ogling happens to be Johnny Depp or George Clooney.

Fly-trap

? *A prospective employer has booked me a business-class ticket to attend a job interview in Australia. I am considering taking my son, because he can stay with grandparents while I attend to business. The airline will change one business fare for two economy seats. Seeing as it involves no extra cost to the company, should I feel any need to advise them of my amendments?*

It depends on why the company is flying you business class. Is it because the prospective employer wouldn't want to insult you by suggesting that you go economy? Or because it wants you to be as rested as possible so that it might better assess your potential as a colleague?

If the latter, then travelling in coach class may not only dent your chances of landing the job (unless you don't want it anyway, in which case it is unethical to tap a company for a fare just so your son can visit his grandparents); it might also mean that the firm has wasted its cash, because it will not be judging you on peak form and may reject someone it should be hiring. But if the company is comping you a business fare merely because it wants to seem generous, why stop at milking it for two economy seats instead? Why not announce that your concerns about global warming make you uneasy about flying all that way just for an interview which can be conducted as easily via live computer links – but, hey, since they would be happy to pay for a flight, you'd be happy for them to deposit an equivalent sum in your bank account?

Logically, that would be OK. Ethically, it would stink. Logically, swapping your business fare for two in economy is a tempting option that many of us would seize. Ethically, it leaves a bad taste: if it didn't, would you think twice about revealing your intentions to the company?

My cup runneth over

While waiting to play five-a-side football at the local leisure centre I noticed that a catering pack of disposable polystyrene cups had been left out. These cups would be useful to me as a teacher, to use in my classroom as paint pots and glue pots. Both the leisure centre and my school are financed by the Government, so would it be stealing if I took a few cups?

Whatever happened to jam jars? Maybe they are all being dutifully recycled by councils that have been set stiff recycling targets that they must meet on pain of government sanctions; such as having to take the Blairs on holiday with them after they've left Downing Street and Cliff Richard and the Bee Gees no longer invite them to stay in their sun-blessed villas.

I'm not sure that if I were a jam jar I wouldn't rather be recycled as a paint pot in a primary school art room, playing my modest part in the creation of paintings that (at least until the Blu-Tack at the corners finally gives out, resulting in the sheets of gaily coloured art-room paper gusting down like autumn leaves to a watery grave in the kitchen sink) are more indulgently admired by the creators' parents than anything Rubens painted. That would be so much jollier than ending up in a council's grim recycling facility, wouldn't it?

Helping yourself to those cups amounts to procurement by warped syllogism: the cups belong to the State; my school belongs to the State; so the cups belong to my school. The leisure centre's towels are paid for by the Government, too; so take a few for art-room rags while you're at it. I guess it's certainly an enterprising way of speeding up Whitehall's cumbersome supplies-requisitioning procedure. I'm using the word 'enterprising' in its sense of 'larcenous'.

A real gas-bag!

I get on with everybody in my open-plan office except for one woman, whose rudeness to me has been noticed by colleagues and our human resources manager. The woman has now raised her animosity to a new level by passing wind when she passes my desk! How she manages this beats me; I certainly can't do that to order. Am I right to be more concerned about gas than words?

Are you sure about this? I've never heard of anyone deliberately expressing their dislike of a work colleague by way of gas emissions. More likely is that your co-worker just happens to be very productive when it comes to wind generation and you are an unhappy beneficiary.

Jerusalem artichokes are in season, and delicious, and may be to blame. Or your colleague may recently have adopted a vegan diet for health or ecology reasons. Switching to such a diet can apparently result in the creation of half a litre of gas a day; which is paradoxical given that environmentally-concerned people often switch to a vegan diet because they deem cows an eco-menace not only on account of their requiring acres of pasture to feed on but also because they produce clouds of methane, a gas every bit as toxic to the planet as the burning of fossil fuels.

Mentioning someone's gas output is impolite. But your colleague might be grateful to be alerted to new pants, invented in America, which hide flatulence. The 'Under-Ease' pants have a filter (made from odour-absorbing charcoal, felt and fibreglass wool) positioned at the gas's exit point.

Or maybe this woman is so glum about sharing an office with you that she's in training to become a modern-day *Le Petomane* (the stage name of Joseph Pujol, the Frenchman who turned Nature's trumpet into a famous stage act) and aims to quit as soon as she finds a circus that will hire her.

A degree of debt

Due to a clerical error, I have been undercharged by around £200 on my bill for university accommodation this term. I'm at my overdraft limit and could do with the money. But I worry that by not paying it I may be disadvantaging other students. Should I come clean and tell the university how much I really owe, or keep quiet and hope I slip under the radar undetected?

Whatever they say about today's universities producing young men and women woefully unprepared to cope with the world of work is evidently nonsense. It's true that most students emerge from university with heads full of useless facts; like the dates of battles, mathematical formulae they'll never use, and a grasp of why it is that oxygen plays so hard to get that hydrogen atoms have to offer themselves in pairs to stand any chance of hitching up with a single oxygen atom (oxygen's the kinky element in the Periodic Table).

But in you they have instilled everything a person needs in order to know how to prosper in the workplace: keep quiet and hope you slip under the radar undetected. A big percentage of working life consists of keeping quiet and hoping you slip under the radar. A workplace comprises tens, maybe hundreds, of people, each of whom is constantly wondering when they'll be found out as charlatans who have no more idea how to do their job than a hippo knows how to do a backflip. In amongst them there'll be a handful of people who are supremely confident that they know how to do their job expertly. These are usually the very people their colleagues consider the most preposterously incompetent.

So, keeping quiet and slipping under the radar is a very useful skill. But, oh yes, I just remembered – not when it comes to paying bills; in which instance it is considered illegal.

4 On The Road

'It is easier to find a traveling companion than to get rid of one'

Art Buchwald

Sandwich course

On holiday in a five-star hotel in Tunisia, several guests were making up rolls and taking other snacks for their lunch. They even carried empty bags with them to breakfast in readiness. I found this impolite to the hotel and difficult for the waiters to deal with. Should I have complained to the management and pointed them out? Spoken to them? Ignored it? Or joined in?

Making a packed lunch from the breakfast buffet has become a sort of advance doggy-bag. Lord knows, hotels have tried their best to discourage the practice, short of actually weighing guests in and out of the dining room.

Some hotels describe themselves as offering a 'family welcome', hoping to prompt visitors to behave as they do when breakfasting in their own homes – you know, just grabbing some toast as they dash out of the house on their way to work or school.

Then hotels loaded their breakfast tables with food items people usually eat only at meals such as lunch – poached salmon, ribs of beef, salamis, a cheeseboard – calculating that if guests ate lunch at breakfast, they wouldn't want to eat a replica lunch at lunchtime, and so wouldn't smuggle out meals in their handbags. When that failed, too, hotels just hiked prices and turned a blind eye, letting guests delude themselves that they were hood-winking the management and stealing a bargain; the way some foreign exchange bureaux offer 'no commission' deals, earning their margins instead on plumper buying-and-selling rates.

Still, that's no reason to abuse a hotel's hospitality. Basically, you're overstepping the mark if you're visiting the breakfast buffet pushing a trolley. But as a holidaymaker, it's not your duty to police fellow guests. Seek the hotel's permission and it may even say: 'Join them!'

cottage loaf

Staying in a cottage, for which we had bid at a school fundraising evening, we noticed a webcam in the main bedroom, hidden in a bookshelf and connected to a computer concealed in a cupboard. We laughed and then covered the webcam with a book. Friends say that we under-reacted. Should we have confronted the owners of the cottage, or even gone straight to the police?

It depresses you a little, doesn't it, that the libido of the British might be so low that illicitly-filmed footage of an unknown middle-aged couple having sex under a duvet might count as sexually titillating? You'd think that if the owners of the cottage are computer-literate enough to set up the necessary electronic links between the concealed webcam and their hidden laptop, then they would also have enough technical expertise to trawl the internet for those video clips of Paris Hilton or Pamela Anderson. Apart from anything else, it's such a gamble, isn't it – I mean as a way of accumulating porn footage – when you look at all the people you bump into at the average parents' evening? It might turn out like visiting a lap-dancing club and finding yourself being attentively serenaded by Michael Moore.

It may be that, with school fees now nudging the price of a personal nuclear defence system, the cottage's owners make ends meet by parading themselves nightly on one of those live porn websites, and just hadn't got around to dismantling the equipment before your arrival. Or else they were hoping to raise more funds for the school at next year's fundraiser by auctioning the video of you and your wife (assuming they couldn't raise more from you first, through blackmail). Confront the cottage's owners for an explanation before acting further.

Cabin pressure

Our initial pleasure at being put in the front seats near the door on our flight from Warsaw was soon shattered by the non-stop conversation across the aisle that began on boarding and persisted until Luton. Subjects ranged from birding in Poland to planning strategies required for protection of the environment. I felt like punching him. What should I have done?

It's true that you are more likely to get killed crossing the street than you are from flying. But which would you choose? The fast, brutish end of an SUV slamming into you at 60 mph? Or the slow death of being buckled into an aircraft seat while having to listen to your neighbours drone for four hours on a subject that even Neil Kinnock – who can construct a twenty-minute-long sentence just to ask for a cup of tea – would struggle to keep going for more than an hour?

It's bad enough having to listen to the plane's captain ('Mike here!') interrupting you every ten minutes with updates on what route he's taking (Mike! We don't care! Just get us there!) without having the gaps between Captain Mike's updates filled by inane chatter from nearby passengers. If people were supposed to chatter loudly on planes they wouldn't have invented in-flight movies: they would have set up in-flight debating societies instead. The only thing worse than having to inhale passive conversation is sitting behind a plane passenger who reclines his seat so far back that you wonder if he's expecting you to shampoo his hair.

What to do? Avoid violence. Instead, ask Captain Mike if he can locate a patch of turbulence so choppy that it unleashes the oxygen masks from their overhead compartments, forcing your neighbours finally to muzzle themselves.

Smoking out a Scam

While I was buying two coffees and some chocolate from a Polish barman on a cross-Channel ferry, he said that he appreciated my chatting to him, so would charge me only for the chocolate. In thanks, I offered to buy him a drink. He said that he'd prefer cigarettes, which cost about the same as the coffees. Had I naively helped the barman to steal cigarettes from his employer?

I haven't yet used one of the legendary Polish plumbers who are said now to repair most of the dripping taps and leaking pipes of distressed Londoners. But I would be surprised if they routinely unjammed ballcocks and, before presenting you with the bill, stated that they so appreciated your chatting to them while they worked that they would halve their fee.

It's easy to be generous with other people's money. Did the barman who so magnanimously waived the bill for your coffees have any right to do so? About the same right as an estate agent who is showing you a property has to invite you to help yourself to any suits from the vendor's wardrobe that take your fancy – in the hope that his generosity might seduce you into buying your new house through him (it's enough that estate agents are so generous with the English language that they describe as 'a rare opportunity to shape to a purchaser's taste and imagination' any property that has been derelict since 1962).

You behaved naively; but not mischievously. You acted as though you were returning hospitality, without dwelling on whether it was the barman's to dispense. It's one thing if a publican offers you a drink on the house – it's his house – another if it's a junior barman who's doing the offering. The ferry barman didn't steal cigarettes from his employer. You bought him those. What he stole was two coffees.

A brush with the Law

? *My teenage daughter forgot to pack a hairbrush on holiday. After stopping to buy a new one, she proudly showed me a brush she'd obtained by switching its price tag with that from a cheaper version. Horrified, I was about to make her return it when I reflected that the manager would call the police and ruin her holiday. So we drove on. Was my action reasonable?*

Ethical? No. Understandable? Yes. Reasonable? Possibly.

It's easy to see why your daughter wanted the best hairbrush she could afford (even if she couldn't, technically, afford it without swapping those price tags: a halfway house between paying the correct price and doing a Winona Ryder).

Why? Because hair has become a very big part of our lives. Every other commercial on TV now trumpets a new hair product that will make a woman's hair wavier/straighter/ shinier/bouncier/blonder/browner. If aliens are tuning in to our TV broadcasts they must be saying to themselves: 'You know why Earthlings have never managed to build a spacecraft capable of reaching our galaxy? It's because all their top scientists are too busy developing breakthough treatments for split ends, and perfecting new ways to provide home colour with that convincing salon look.' This kind of pressure can turn a girl's head (or so the shampoo manufacturers promise).

You were right to be horrified; and reasonable not to drag the police into it, since you could have remedied this transgression without taking the law into your own hands. But you were misguided not to have discreetly remedied it – say, by returning the brush to the shop, getting a refund and repurchasing the brush at its correct, higher price. You should have done the right thing. Why? Because you're worth it.

Firmly Seat-belted

Boarding my rush-hour train ten minutes before departure, I spotted a seat occupied only by a suitcase. 'Someone's sitting there,' said a woman in the next seat. I retreated, and watched from the end of the carriage as it became clear that she was waiting for her husband, who boarded the train more than five minutes later. Which of us had the greater claim on that seat?

This dilemma has less to do with ethics than with thickness of skin. A seat reservation would have solved the dispute on the spot. In the absence of such a reservation, you both had legitimate, rival claims to that seat. You, having the less thick skin, graciously conceded.

Your title to the seat is obvious enough. You buy a ticket for a journey, you board the train, you notice an empty seat and you feel you have every right to sit there (this is, of course, not the same thing as saying that because you have paid for a train journey, you have a right to expect a seat on that train for the duration of that journey, a belief that train operating companies regard as being as hilariously fanciful as believing in the tooth fairy).

The woman, too, may have thought that she had a legitimate right to that seat. Without cross-examining her, you have no way of knowing if her husband had been occupying the seat earlier and had gone to buy a newspaper, or to find a lavatory or to make an urgent phone call. Even if the wife had been merely reserving the seat for her husband, we tolerate this convention in most circumstances (in cafés and cinemas, for instance), or else life would become very brutish.

It's always possible that the husband was in the luggage all along, punished by his ferocious wife for some transgression by being made to travel inside the suitcase, like a ventriloquist's dummy.

No taxi-meeter

I booked a minicab to meet me at the airport after a business trip and take me to see my son playing a sports match. The cab wasn't there: the driver phoned to say he was stuck in traffic. He arrived forty-five minutes late and I missed my son's match because I felt morally obliged to wait. Would it have been unethical to take a black cab, leaving the minicab driver without a fare?

If your son's sports match and your wish to treat your traffic-ensnared minicab driver fairly were equally important to you, an obvious answer might have been to jump in a black cab, pay the minicab driver anyway for his trouble, and watch your son thrashing the opposition on the field.

Equally ethical would have been to take a black cab and explain to the minicab why you had to cut and run. It might be unfortunate, but a cab is booked on the understanding that it will collect you at an agreed hour, and deliver you in time to wherever it is you're going. Will your abandoned minicab driver be thrilled to have lost your custom? No. But he will understand that your motive was not malice. If your newsagent failed to deliver your newspaper because the paperboy was off sick, you'd commiserate, but you wouldn't expect him to charge you for the paper, a copy of which you later bought at the station on your way to work.

Of course, your minicab driver might see your abandoning him as a problem. But the great thing about cab drivers is that they know the solution to every problem the world can offer, from choked roads to Chechnya. If only taxi drivers and barbers joined forces, they could run the United Nations in their spare time (HAIRDRESSER: 'Oh, my! Who did you let loose on your Middle East crisis last time! What a mess! Leave it to me. Just need to get it washed first.')

Not fare at all

My mother and I were waiting to catch a ferry. The ferries were running late, and in the rush the ticket collector did not ask for our tickets. My mother did not point out the error, arguing that 'if they forget to ask for my ticket, that is their problem, not mine'. As a result we travelled without paying. Is this acceptable?

There is a big difference between feeling yourself to have been lucky and feeling yourself to be morally in the right because you got away with something: Sylvester Stallone is lucky to have an acting career, but that doesn't make it morally right for him to inflict his movies on us.

Imagine if your mother had lunched with a friend, having agreed to split the cost, but paid the whole bill because her friend needed to visit a bank before contributing her share. What if the friend forgot to find a cashpoint and failed to settle her half of the bill before she and your mother went their separate ways? Would your mother think that such a financial outcome was fair, the onus having been on her to remember to demand the cash from her friend before they parted?

No need to pay for a ferry ticket because the ticket collector was too busy to notice? You might as well say that you're entitled to leave a store with an armful of clothes you haven't paid for if the store's owner is too busy to notice. Your mother might wish to consider herself lucky to have been spared the cost of two ferry tickets, but she can't claim to have acted ethically.

It might feel different, but not buying a ticket is ethically little nobler than dipping your hand into the ticket-seller's moneybag and helping yourself to a tenner.

Feeling cowardly about a room with a view

> As my companion and I were about to leave for a holiday in India, the travel company informed us that, contrary to its brochure, our hotel in Agra would not have a Taj Mahal view – and refunded us £60. On arrival, we found our room did, after all. Should we repay the money?

Repay whom? If the travel firm gets billed by the hotel for a room with a view, it will surely contact you. The hotel may not have charged its usual Taj-Mahal-view supplement through administrative error. But it might also have been genuinely confused as to which price it quoted, because hotels routinely levy a variety of rates for the same room, depending on when you booked, whether you have a corporate deal, if you belong to a loyalty scheme, the whim of the receptionist, and so on.

It's also possible that the hotel had a low occupancy rate when you were visiting Agra and, generously, thought that it would be no skin off its nose to enhance your stay by upgrading you to a room offering a vision of something even more hauntingly white than Michael Jackson's face.

The hotel may have calculated that by putting an extra spring in your step, you might be minded to recommend the hotel to friends also planning trips to Agra (thereby boosting the hotel's future occupancy rate and, in turn, denying your friends the chance of the very sort of room upgrade that prompted you to praise the hotel to them in the first place. A cute paradox).

One way to have repaid the hotel would have been by tipping generously during your stay. If you failed to do that, you should at least write a letter gushing about how much you enjoyed your visit. The hotel manager can then pin your letter to the staff noticeboard, annotated with the words: 'Remember the cheap tippers? They're hoping this letter will make up for it.'

check it out, big boy!

When boarding a plane recently I was charged £10 for exceeding the permitted luggage limit. However, the chap beside me on the flight was at least three times my size and was carrying on board significantly more additional weight than my measly two extra kilos. Should he be charged for his excess weight?

Plane tickets are sold on a similar basis to all-you-can-eat buffets. Some people pay the fixed price for their meal and barely nibble a carrot, while others eat their own bodyweight in puddings alone. The restaurant works out how much food it is likely to sell, to how many diners, then prices its fixed-price tariff accordingly.

Where the restaurant makes its money is on the drinks. The drinks bill is the restaurant equivalent of an airline's luggage surcharge. Stick to tap water (or your luggage allowance) and you get to eat (or fly) at the advertised fare. Order champagne (or pack enough to see Elton John through a season's worth of costume changes in Las Vegas) and you pay a surcharge.

You can't carry over a notional credit, gained from being lighter than the average passenger, to your luggage allowance. To charge your fellow passenger for being heavier than you would be as unfair as levying a linen laundry surcharge on a messy diner. Try thinking more positively about your fellow flyer. He's probably at his ideal weight: just a couple of feet shorter than his ideal height.

Guide price

At an exhibition in Paris, a group of English students was receiving a lecture. The strength of the lecturer's voice, combined with good acoustics in a small area, meant that it was difficult not to get caught up in what she was saying. A man reprimanded me, saying: 'You do know this is a private party!' Yet I too had paid to see the exhibition. Was my eavesdropping unethical?

When you wander around a cathedral abroad, squinting at the frescoes and stained glass, strolling past clots of tourists being lectured to in German or Spanish or Japanese, and you suddenly hear a guide speaking English, you can't help but ingest what is being said. It's like swivelling the dial of a radio and suddenly tuning in to a channel as opposed to white noise.

Providing you were not nudging your way to the front of the party, it's hard to see what was so shameful about your behaviour. Those in the private party were not inconvenienced by your sharing their education. Their lecturer said no more and no less than she otherwise would.

It's similar to slotting a two-euro coin into one of those machines in Italian churches to illuminate a dimly-lit canvas: you can't force everyone else in the vicinity of the painting to shield their eyes while you exclusively enjoy your €2 worth of wattage. Bystanders sharing the benefit of your two euros costs you nothing extra; which is a cheap price to pay for spreading some joy and enlightenment to others.

The man who chided you was mean-spirited. Would you ban strangers from listening to songs you've paid for on a jukebox, or from looking out of their windows at your fireworks display? You could have complained that your silent contemplation was being frayed by his loud lecturer.

Trophy room

Attempting to book our dream hotel in the Caribbean, and told that it was full, my husband expressed surprise that it was harder to get a room than for his wife to win an Oscar. With this throwaway remark the hotel miraculously found us a room. I have never worked in the film business (though he does), haven't won an Oscar this year, and won't next year. When confirming the room, do I confess?

First point: can you actually be thought to have behaved unethically towards a hotel that is minded to let rooms only to the famous, rather than to open its doors to anyone who books early enough and who can afford to pay the hotel's room rates? It's not even as if your husband lied: it was the hotel's lust for a starry guest list that led it to hoodwink itself.

If that gives you the moral confidence, or at least the brazenness, not to put the hotel straight with regard to your Oscar tally, then it's very unlikely that you'll be found out. For one thing, you could have been the toast of Hollywood when your husband booked, and be unknown again by next Christmas, what with modern celebrity having roughly the same shelf life as milk.

If you do receive sceptical squints when you arrive, and someone on the hotel staff is brassy enough to press you on the point, you could always suggest that you were up for an Oscar in one of those categories so recondite ('Best music soundtrack on a foreign animated short film not featuring the voice of Robin Williams') that they don't even bother to show it on the Oscars TV coverage. Or the hotel staff might not recognise you, but still give you the benefit of the doubt, being well aware that Hollywood is an ever-changing gallery of new faces – even if most of them are on the same old people as before.

That's the Limit!

? *Is it morally correct for a driver in the offside (overtaking) lane on a motorway, who is driving at 70mph, not to let the car behind overtake, given that he is himself already driving at the legal limit?*

As soon as you try to insert the word 'law' into any sentence it makes everything more complicated, a bit like hosing an issue with slurry. That's how lawyers come to earn handsome salaries; and also how Richard Nixon managed to stroll out of the White House a free man.

But there is a difference between not breaking the law and preventing someone else from breaking the law. I mean, where would you draw the line? If you spotted someone in a striped T-shirt, wearing a Lone Ranger eye mask, carrying a sack marked 'swag', and climbing up a ladder into a bedroom window, you might well be prompted to phone the police (they might not show up, of course; although they might offer you counselling to relieve any trauma you suffered as a result of having witnessed a burglary in progress). But do you saunter around a pub to check whether patrons have drunk too much to drive home within the legal drink-drive limit?

There is a limit to our civic obligations; as well as to how much we can be bothered to interfere in other people's business to prevent their potentially committing an offence. There is a difference between witnessing a man breaking into a car and spotting a man who looks shifty; and between a driver doing 120mph down a country lane and one doing 70mph on a motorway who might speed up if you move out of his way – possibly to 120mph, possibly to only 74mph. If we always assume the worst, we might as well never release anyone from prison who has been banged up, say, four times for the same crime, on the ground that the odds are that they will just do the same thing again.

Extra! Extra! Read all about it!

While backpacking in Vietnam, we hired a boat for a day through an agency. The unpleasant driver tried to overcharge us for 'extras' and insisted on being back within four hours. Were we right to complain? He lived on the boat with three children and was obviously very poor, so we didn't want him to lose his job. But we felt a duty to protect future tourists.

When visiting a country where earnings and living costs are both much lower than in your homeland, you might feel torn between feeling guilt at spending as much on a hotel room for one night as the hotel chambermaids earn in a month, and enjoying the fruits of your comparative wealth by, say, hiring taxis for a full day, always ordering the lobster, and – why not? They're so cheap! – wondering if it would really be so unethical to buy a couple of the natives to take home, too.

But it's not your duty to set the prices of goods and services in the world marketplace. It's (mostly) the responsibility of the marketplace – though if you can afford it, there is certainly no shame, when visiting a poor region, in erring on the side of generosity when hiring a boatman, or tipping a waiter. But nor is it ethical for a boatman, or waiter, to blackmail tourists into just handing them wads of cash out of pity, or through threats of delivering poorer service to those they deem stingy.

By staining Vietnam's reputation among tourists, your boatman did himself and his countrymen a disservice, since if his behaviour results in fewer visitors to his region, he will be worse off than he is already. So, ethically, you were right to complain. But that's not to say that many of us, in similar circumstances, might not have had the stomach to do so.

Feeling Snappy

When visiting tourist sites, I like to wander around, taking it all in. But my enjoyment is constantly interrupted by people taking photographs. Am I duty bound to keep watching them closely, so that I avoid walking in front of them during a snapshot, or should I let them do it at their own risk?

Many tourists have corrupted Descartes' remark, 'I think, therefore I am', into, 'I photographed, therefore I was there'. Or maybe they're guided by the maxim, 'Justice should not only be done, but should be seen to be done', but twisting it into, 'Venice should not only be visited, but should be seen to have been visited'. (To which you might coin an alternative, such as 'Some tourist behaviour must not only be done, it must be seen to be believed'.) It's not as if many of their photos are worth taking. You notice tourists, with endearing optimism, pointing their disposable cameras at a stained-glass window sixty metres away to capture an image that will turn out to be roughly one-thousandth as enlightening as the same scene being sold on a postcard in the souvenir kiosk.

Many tourists have barely enough time to take a photo in a church or a museum before their guide speeds them on to the next masterpiece. They return home having never seen any painting, cloister or statue with their naked eye, only through the fisheye lens in their camera. If Michelangelo and Leonardo had only known, they could have polished off their

David and Mona Lisa without fretting over every last detail.

Keeping out of tourists' photographs is a courtesy, not a moral duty. Aim to err on the side of generosity, unless this means standing in one spot for the whole of your holiday – which, in St Mark's Square, it might.

Emergency measures

> **?** *When driving, I have always made way for police cars rushing to emergencies. But recently police resources in my area have been diverted from tackling crime to apparently political tasks. I feel strongly about our long-held freedoms. Should I continue to give way to police cars that may be merely on their way to arrest someone trying to exercise their right to free speech?*

Just imagine how different the world might be if Mahatma Gandhi and Martin Luther King had sensed the civil disobedience potential of not pulling their cars over to the side of the road whenever they heard a police siren wailing like an angry electronic baby behind them.

Instead of that uninspiring, forgettable speech he delivered, Martin Luther King could have planted some real political fire into the bellies of millions of Americans had he said, instead: 'I have a dream that, when driving in their cars, the people of this nation will not turn on their indicators and meekly pull over towards the kerb whenever they hear a siren indicating that a police car wants to overtake them, possibly en route to an emergency: we hold these truths to be self-evident, that all road-users are created equal. I have a dream.'

You have every right, and good reason, to feel strongly about our long-held freedoms. But is obstructing a police car –

on the high-risk hunch that the police might be going not to catch criminals but, rather, to arrest someone for chanting slogans outside 10 Downing Street – really the most effective way to voice your protest? How long would it take for politicians to be even aware of your grievance, let alone to work out what it might be? It's like protesting against the logging of rainforests by refusing to prune the apple tree in your back garden.

Hello? Yeah, I'm in my cab!

I was travelling in a cab when the driver took a call on his personal mobile. He removed a hand from the wheel to chat and, when negotiating a roundabout, took his other hand off the wheel to change gear. Should I have asked him to end the call . . . quietly indicated disapproval . . . or complained to his firm? In taking no action, was I an accessory to a criminal offence?

It's understandable to feel slightly anxious about interrupting a taxi driver when he receives an urgent call on his mobile phone. That's because you feel that you can never rule out the possibility that it might be Tony Blair or George Bush or Vladimir Putin on the line, seeking advice on how to tackle a crisis that has just arisen – what with most cabbies seeming to have a sixth sense about how to cure most of the world's problems. You sometimes wonder whether people in MI6 and the Treasury are working undercover as London cabbies, serving as a mobile force of experts ready to resolve any diplomatic or economic crisis (providing, obviously, that the crisis doesn't erupt south of the river).

Cabbies also test their passengers' defiance. For instance,

they've now increased fares to a level where they know they must be picking up passengers so desperate to avoid using public transport that a cabbie could play Celine Dion CDs and his passenger would still be too cowed to protest.

But yours was driving dangerously. If you were reluctant to risk being turfed out by complaining to his face, you could have complained to his firm. You were not criminally culpable. But if your inaction results in more cabbies fearlessly playing Celine Dion songs, your inertia could have criminal consequences.

Roundabout route to the office

? *When commuting to work, I face a huge queue to turn right at a roundabout. The left-hand lane is usually almost empty and some drivers use this to get to the roundabout. They then turn left into a tiny lane and do a U-turn to regain access to the roundabout. It's blatant queue-jumping, but not illegal. Should I follow suit?*

Are you wrestling with your conscience, or embarrassed about what other drivers think of you? Because if it's the latter, don't bother. I can tell you what they think, and I've never even met you. They think you're an idiot. Drivers think all other drivers are idiots. Well, not all idiots, obviously. Some are morons. But you never hear a driver say, 'Look at that maroon car! Did you see how beautifully he changed lanes?'

Short cuts are subject to the laws of science. Just as water finds its own level, any short cut quickly gets exploited by so many that the old long cut becomes the new short cut. Then the authorities find out about the old short cut and erect a sign prohibiting drivers from using it. With nobody now using the old short cut, the old long cut becomes the longer cut. You see?

By trying to save time, you lengthen your journey. It's all orchestrated by the Driving God, to make sure you never enjoy a journey.

In the road marketplace, as in any market, knowledge is king. There's nothing morally wrong with exploiting local street knowledge. It's a bonus we each enjoy in our own neighbourhoods. Just don't expect to enjoy it for long. Or to be loved by other drivers while you're using it.

Welsh penalty

While driving with a friend to North Wales for a walking weekend, I was caught speeding through Llangollen. My friend has sent me a lovely framed photograph of our weekend's epic route, plus a cheque for half the fine, stating that it was a fifty-fifty choice as to who should drive. Should I return his cheque?

You have to recognise that there's a certain paradox in being caught speeding en route to a leisurely walking weekend in Wales, where the pleasure comes from ambling across the countryside, the better to appreciate the spectacular views. It's like those people who drive two miles to a gym then spend an hour pacing monotonously on a walking machine while they either squint at a TV monitor showing an episode of *Friends* with the volume turned off, or else watch sweat drizzle out of a stranger's crotch on to the seat of the rowing machine that they were thinking of using but which, on further reflection, they will now be giving a miss.

Your friend is being generous in offering to split the cost of the fine. Possibly, he was spurred to do so by unwarranted feelings of guilt. Unless he was urging you to put your foot down in order to reach your destination more quickly, he wasn't a partner to the crime; just a bystander. You were certainly noble in offering to do the driving, but that doesn't mean you can blame your passenger for your errors. Your friend is no more responsible for your breaking the speed limit than you would be for suffering food poisoning if you were to accept his offer to prepare dinner and he neglected to cook the chicken thoroughly.

Return his cheque. If he is too decent a friend to accept it, spend it on a good bottle you can share.

Exhausted by country life

I recently revisited friends who have moved to the country. Hunting for the sign that I'd followed on my first visit to their remote farmhouse, I caused £120-worth of damage to my exhaust while scrambling over a concrete ridge across a driveway. Since they had failed to tell me in advance that farmers had knocked down the sign, should my friends have offered to contribute to the repair bill?

It's easy enough to see why you might feel aggrieved by the reticence of your hosts. But chastising people who live in the countryside can leave a bad taste in the mouth: it can feel like kicking a man when he's down. You sense that country folk are already suffering enough by finding themselves living in a place where the residents have traditionally been so unfriendly that they have made a point of building their houses as far away from each others' as possible. Is that cosy?

That's why country-dwellers who are thinking of moving to another house can make prickly customers for estate agents: they are often minded to slap an agent who happens to take them to view a property from which you can even see another house.

So it's possible that your friends only barely registered that the sign to their farmhouse was no longer there. Country-dwellers take a while to notice anything – unless maybe it has big udders. And those udders are sore.

Either way, we cannot hold others to account for our own driving errors. It is not their obligation to map our route, merely a kindness. For many rural types who are deprived of cinemas, restaurants and the scary hilarity of living under Ken Livingstone's mayoral regime in London, locating hard-to-find houses situated in the wilds of the countryside counts as entertainment.

Short change

Though sixteen years old, I am short for my age, and look younger. So when I buy a train ticket, I am often charged a child rate even though, at sixteen, I should pay an adult fare. I never specify what kind of ticket I need, and the clerks assume my age incorrectly. Should I correct them and reveal that I should pay the full fare at my age, or assume it is their mistake?

It is true that adults hardly set a good example in the area of keeping a low profile and hoping that nobody will ask awkward questions that might expose them as charlatans and frauds. Politicians, in particular, are famous for hoping that, if they keep their lips sealed, the public might give them the benefit of the doubt, and might imagine even that they have insightful contributions to make should a major national debate arise. Then a major national debate arises and Clare Short gets up to speak and blows the cover for the lot of them.

Some people think that a smart course through life is to do nothing and to say less; which is fine if you are an amoeba. Otherwise, it can be construed as a form of calculated deception. For instance, Arnold Schwarzenegger, the Governor of California, may be non-committal about whether he'll return to making movies if voted out of office as a shrewd way of keeping people voting for him.

Not lying to a train-ticket-seller about your age does not make you any less guilty of having defrauded the train company than a criminal who doesn't confess to a crime, or who doesn't hand himself in to the nearest police station, would be not guilty of having broken the law. You aren't innocent; it's just that you haven't been found out. You might as well say that Everest was not the tallest mountain in the world until it was measured by Sir George Everest.

Free to roam

Working in the media, I sometimes get free trips. I invited a friend on a trip in which she got a free hotel room, meals and some exciting excursions because she was with me. Did I expect too much in hoping that she might treat me to a cup of tea, or to a drink, in return? I would have, were I in her shoes. Should I ditch my friend, or lower my expectations?

What philosophers often fail to grasp is that the question to which people most frequently seek the answer is not 'Does God exist?', or 'Why are we here?', but rather 'Is it free?'

Yet paying has its uses. Price is the market's trick for balancing supply of a product or a service with demand for it. Without price, a market is left confused. Mark Twain said that if, when riding a bicycle, you try to run over a dog, it knows how to calculate. But if you're trying to miss him he doesn't know how to calculate and is liable to jump the wrong way every time. Equally, if you pitch a firm price, the market knows whether to buy or sell. If you offer something free, people struggle to work out if they can be bothered even to take it from you.

When we get something for nothing, we may not activate that part of our brain that computes value for money (as we might if we'd spent £40 to see a play that was as riveting as watching photosynthesis) – unless we happen to be enjoying something free only because, say, our host is treating us, in which case we are duly appreciative. Aware that you didn't pay for her trip, your friend may not have bothered valuing it, and thus may not have felt obligated to you. She's not immoral; just ungracious.

Sorry camp sight

> *While camping with friends, I accidentally broke a canvas chair belonging to them. The chair was sold as a set of two. My wife and I offered to buy a new set, but our friends insisted that we replace only the broken chair. What should happen?*

What should happen? Primarily, what should happen is that you should stop going camping. You should count yourself lucky that you managed to get away so lightly, with only a broken canvas chair to cast a shadow over events. Because the sort of people who willingly go camping often turn out to be the sort of people who probably shouldn't be allowed to operate heavy machinery even before they've taken the sort of medication that makes you go drowsy.

To non-campers, the appeal of sleeping outdoors and cooking meals on teensy stoves that emit the same heat as a vapour rub is baffling. Even more baffling to non-campers is that people nowadays actually book in advance to secure a spot in the more popular campsites so as not to be disappointed on arrival – just for the opportunity to sleep under a thin piece of cloth in the open air, 400 metres from a lavatory. How moving from sleeping in caves, which offer protection from wind and rain, to sleeping in the open air came to be counted as an advance in civilisation is a bigger mystery to most people than Fermat's Last Theorem.

I think your friend knows that having matching furniture doesn't figure all that high on campsite etiquette. It was generous of you to offer even to replace the broken chair, but your friend wasn't obliged to accept the offer. Since he has, you should fit in with his plans.

crash course

On holiday I shared the hire of a car with a friend: as passenger, not driver. One day she left the handbrake off when parking, damaging another car. I learnt that she had waived the insurer's excess charge, so the bill came to £600. I consider both the accident and her decision to waive the excess cover to be her responsibility. She contends that we should share the £600.

It's possible that your friend didn't deliberately choose to skip on the extra insurance. After a long flight, with nothing to sustain you apart from movies starring Demi Moore and meals that taste like a steam-heated buoyancy aid, it's always confusing when you collect a pre-paid rental car ('Yes, it comes with unlimited mileage and insurance' – ha-ha-ha! The industry's little joke!) to find the local agent asking whether you want a collision-damage waiver. And excess waiver. Oh yes, and theft waiver, and theft-excess waiver, and extra driver, and that insurance you have to take out to valet the seats if melting ice-cream drips on them.

But even if your friend chose to economise, you should still share the consequences of her decision. Just as it is no defence, when you break a law, to say you weren't aware that there was even a law to break ('Your Honour, you mean that shooting my neighbour was wrong?'), so it is awkward to argue that you're not responsible for contributing to any excess on the car hire because your friend had not alerted you that she was skimping on insurance.

It was your responsibility to ask whether she had bought all the available insurance cover, if that was something important to you. When we don't ask questions, we bear the consequences, which is a painful aspect of life whether we're renting a car or electing an MP.

Thai knot

? *Our local education authority allows pupils to be taken out of school for up to ten days. After I had bought flights to attend a wedding in Thailand at Christmas, requiring my seven-year-old son to miss eight days of school, his school switched to a policy of banning all absences in term time. As a governor of my son's school, would it be unethical to continue with my plans?*

At the age of seven, what exactly is your son likely to miss in the eight days preceding the Christmas holidays? A bit of

Christmas decoration-making? A carol concert? A few afternoons spent laboriously turning an egg carton, some quick-dry clay, four mismatched buttons, a pipe-cleaner and some paint into a Christmas present for his parents, which they will then dutifully have to display in their sitting room until at least February for fear of hurting his feelings?

And what will he gain by joining you in Thailand instead? A glimpse of stunning temples; a taste of exquisite food; an opportunity to risk his life sitting in the back of a tuk-tuk, a form of transport that might result in a far greater number of casualties if Bangkok's traffic ever manages to move faster than a lame tortoise. Oh, yes, and the chance to walk through parts of Bangkok at an age when he is is still unaware that some of the women he is walking past can expel smoke rings from orifices he doesn't yet know even exist; or, indeed, that some of the women he is walking past are not even actual women.

You have not broken any school rules. You would be transgressing only if you booked your holiday now. Nor could any parent accuse you of having abused your position as a governor to bend the rules. Though it is attractive to behave ethically, it can be unattractive to try to behave too ethically.

Tree Line

? *It is now fashionable for people to excuse their heavy use of, say, plane travel by declaring that they plant a sufficient number of trees to render their jet journeys 'carbon neutral'. Does that make it OK for me to behave immorally (but not illegally) as long as I, say, donate a compensating sum to charity to make my moral transgression 'ethically neutral'?*

Many of us remain a little hazy on the mechanics of precisely how carbon-offsetting reduces the amount of greenhouse gases in the atmosphere. Isn't flying around the world and then planting six trees to restore the balance of Nature a bit like a man killing another human being and then redressing the world's population imbalance by impregnating a woman at random?

Maybe the idea is simply that when enough trees are planted in carbon-offset programmes there won't be room left on the planet to build roads for petrol-burning cars to drive along, and no remaining patch of land large enough to create an aeroplane runway. Is that how it works?

By contrast, the practice of behaving immorally and then donating a compensating sum to charity, or to a good cause, so as to render your moral transgression 'ethically neutral', has a long tradition. People donate to charity as a form of credit on their celestial bank account, hoping to put themselves back into credit after having slipped, ethically-speaking, into the red. There are also ethical 'savers' – people who donate to charity not because they've misbehaved, but because they find it reassuring to know that they have credit in their account should they stray next Tuesday. In this sense, charity-giving lies somewhere between seeking forgiveness for having misbehaved and buying yourself good luck en route to an appointment with your cardiologist.

Snow flake

> *Friends who rented a ski chalet for Easter have a bedroom spare and invited me to join them. The time has come for them to pay the final balance. But I am unwilling to commit, for fear there might be no snow come Easter. If I don't go, the spare room will remain empty, at no cost to my friends. But some of them feel I am taking advantage by keeping my options open. Am I?*

When it comes to matters of money, logic can sometimes slip away for a holiday. Logic would suggest that a waiter should be tipped a fixed sum for serving you in a restaurant. Whether he hands you a starter of caviar costing £80, or some liver pâté costing a fiver, it involves the same amount of fetching and carrying from the kitchen. It takes the same effort to pour you a £20 bottle of wine as it does a £200 bottle. But a waiter's tip swells in proportion with your final bill. Does that make sense? No, not really. If anything a restaurant should be subsidising your service charge to encourage you to order its most expensive dishes and priciest clarets. But would you wish to debate this logic with your waiter? No, not really.

Your (by now, possibly, former) friends evidently feel that you are milking their generosity, and their willingness to make the early commitment needed to secure a good chalet, by offering to pay your share only at the last minute – should you belatedly decide to join them on the piste after all. Your logic is impeccable (if you don't go, the room will just remain empty, neither increasing nor reducing your friends' outlay, so why the fuss?); but your manners and morals are wanting. By your logic, if you do decide to go, why should you pay anything at all, since you'd be using a room whose cost your chalet-bookers had already written off?

Save-a-ticket

> **?** *If I sit in the last train carriage, there is an 80 per cent chance that the guard will not get to me before I disembark. If he does reach me, I must pay him the full 'flexible fare', which is nearly double that of the 'saver' ticket I could buy if I endured the queues and unreliable ticket machines on the concourse. My lawyer says I'm not doing anything wrong. Am I?*

Lord knows, train companies make it hard for passengers to work out the price of any journey. Fares seem to vary depending on the time of day, the weather, the Queen's mood, tidal movements, gravity, Hollywood box-office takings, sun-spot cycles and how big a breakfast the stationmaster has had. The only people who recite numbers more randomly than train-ticket-sellers are bingo callers. The chances of two passengers having paid the same fare for the same journey are really pretty much the same as the chances of Elton John becoming the next Pope.

Even so – you'd better sit down: this might jolt you – the reason the fare paid on board a train is twice that of buying the same ticket at the station is to encourage passengers to buy that ticket before boarding. It's not priced at a ratio of two-to-one so as to replicate the odds of a racetrack gamble, spurring you to weigh up your chances of either travelling free or else paying twice the ticket-office price, depending on how lucky you felt at the time.

As for your lawyer: did he come via a recommendation from Tony Soprano? The idea that you are behaving lawfully (let alone ethically) when you avoid paying because you'd be very willing to pay if an inspector asked you to do so? That's as fanciful as saying you behave lawfully if you sneak out of a restaurant without paying so long as the waiter hasn't noticed you've done a runner.

Solving a wee problem

? *I own holiday accommodation in which the beds have duvets. When a duvet is peed on (about three times a year), is it more environment-friendly to launder it – a fourteen-mile drive to use a commercial washing machine, consuming petrol, electricity, water that costs me £8 and two hours – or to bulk-buy cheap new duvets, which requires one twenty-two-mile trip but adds to landfill?*

Did you really have to give away the trade secrets of a holiday accommodation landlady? We will never again be able to enjoy a night in a bed-and-breakfast without sweatily wondering whether we have inherited a duvet which has been weed on, but whose owner has not been as hygienically scrupulous as you evidently are.

So in that sense, it's obviously much, much better, duvet-wise, to have been weed on and washed, than never to have been washed at all. But would you be serving the environment more nobly by avoiding the fourteen-mile car journey, along with saving all the electricity and water needed for the washing machine, and just buying a few new duvets? As a queasy customer, I'd vote for the new duvet. If I were being more environmentally considerate, I might have to plump for the less-wasteful wash-and-reuse option.

Though buying cheap, new (presumably polyester-filled) duvets might save on petrol and electricity in the short run, it inevitably creates a longer-term demand for factories to make more duvets, requiring more swollen polyester padding, and creating more future landfill. It's not as if such duvets have any recycling potential. There's little you can do with a polyester-stuffed duvet, apart from reheating the filling in small tinfoil containers and serving it up as airline food.

Fast gaining currency

Whilst on holiday, we wanted to change £40 at a local street bureau de change. A man who was about to open the office exchanged our sterling with notes from his pocket. Later checking the money, I found that in his haste to do a trade for himself rather than through the books, he'd given us £100-worth of local currency, not £40. Should we have profited from his dishonesty?

You have stumbled upon one of the serendipitous joys of exchange rates. Little has made Europe duller than the introduction of the Euro, a bland currency which has not only blunted many of the continent's economies, but also denied us the thrill we used to get when crossing from Italy into neighbouring countries and being unable to buy breakfast with our unspent lire on account of the rest of Europe regarding all Italian banknotes as fit for use only as kindling.

The other quirk of exchange rates is that they are usually quoted in sufficiently complex ratios to make quick mental arithmetic tricky.

However, milking this confusion in currency rates is a

fruitful source of revenue for international money traders, who exploit even minor discrepancies in exchange rates by, for instance, switching billions of yen into sterling and then switching that sterling into dollars and then the dollars back into yen, in order to end up with more billions of yen than they started out with. It's the nearest the world gets to manufacturing money out of thin air like a magician: it's the currency world's equivalent of Lewis Carroll's mythical island where everyone made a precarious living taking in each other's washing. What's more, it's entirely legal! Whereas backstreet currency-trading is not. But have you considered a career in international currency trading? You seem to have a knack for it.

5 Money (really) Matters

'I started out with nothing and I've still got most of it left'

Groucho Marx

Got it taped

> **?** *Is it unethical for me to tape-record CDs borrowed from my local library? The library still has the CD to lend to others, and I am not depriving anyone of profit, since I have little money: so, given no alternative, I would do without rather than buy the CD anyway. This practice might not suit record companies or the recording artists, but does that make it wrong?*

It's becoming tricky to get anyone to pay for anything any more. Everyone is so used to downloading everything for free from the internet, legally or illegally, that they find the idea of anyone actually charging them for anything a bit of an affront. But the reason everything is free on the net is that every page you turn to is embroidered with banner ads, which supposedly fund the cost of running the site. Pretty soon someone will realise that there is nobody earning money to go out and buy any of the goods that are being plugged in all those little adverts because everyone is at home watching, reading and listening to things for free on the internet. They don't need money any more. The only things web-surfers can't get for free is clothes, and they don't need those because they're at home staring at their computers all day, scouring the internet. In fact, some of those pages probably require that they *don't* wear any clothes.

So when you say the library still has the CD, and that you're not hurting anyone's profit because you wouldn't buy the CD anyway, it's hard to fault you without sounding churlish. But I'm not a recording artist, or a record company. Even if I were, I think I would factor into my income forecasts that some people will be taping CDs they borrowed from libraries or from friends. Just so long as you're not also running a business re-selling your tape recordings on the net. To people who surf the web naked. And who always have their webcam switched on.

On the shelf

When my wife buys pre-packed perishable products from a supermarket, she rummages at the back of the shelf for the later dated items, even if the front ones are OK for our needs. I am uneasy about this. If everybody did it, the shop would have to sell the stuff more cheaply or throw it away.

Tony Curtis says he wouldn't be caught dead married to a woman old enough to be his wife. When an ageing Frank Sinatra took up with Mia Farrow, Dean Martin joked that he had a whisky at home older than his buddy's latest bride. To Anna Nicole Smith, a ninety-year-old millionaire turned out to be a hot little biscuit. People have their own instinctive sense of how old is too old in something that they're eyeing up, whether it's a fresh partner or a fresh steak.

There was a time when sell-by dates weren't attached to anything (which explains Jim Davidson's jokes). People would buy food and decide when it was no longer fit to eat; usually when it was hosting a colony of bacteria big enough to merit its own rail network. Then supermarkets began pre-packing foods, attaching labels detailing their price and by when they should be eaten. Shoppers began following this advice religiously, even though it was being provided by the same supermarket bosses who were also trying to persuade them that it was healthy to buy cheese that came in a tube, and raw chicken breasts the colour of cigarette ash.

If it's on the shop shelf, I think your wife is entitled to choose it. Other shoppers may even prefer their taramasalata or T-bone with a bit more of a well-aged tang about them. Moreover, shoppers hunting for discounted end-of-shelf-life bargains may need a financial break, so your wife may even be helping to spread some cheer, even if it isn't exactly hers to spread.

chickening out

> **?** *We have been invited to the wedding of a wealthy couple. We are not well off. They have sent everyone a form inviting donations of such gifts as chickens to the Third World. Must we cough up handsomely, or can we give a more modest amount than would have been the case were the couple struggling to set up home?*

The etiquette of present-giving has become pretty relaxed. Partly this is because people have become rich enough to be able to afford most trinkets they want; partly because when you see the sort of trinkets on sale in gift shops you realise that people will now apparently accept anything. The exception remains Japan, a country where it is never just the thought that counts, and where the codes and conventions of what to give, when to give it, and to whom, remain more complex than the kind of algebra that would have given even Wittgenstein a headache.

The basic rule when you're at the receiving end of a present is that any gift is generous, and no gift too small. If someone is going to adjust their opinion of you as a result of the present you bought them, they invited you to their party for the wrong reason (that goes even if what you bought them was a gift voucher to spend at Don King's hairdresser).

Being rich, your hosts have sensibly decided that it's best not to clutter their house with unwanted toasters and vases. And being thoughtful, they have offered anyone still keen to celebrate their marriage an opportunity to donate something to needy Third World communities. This couple's attitude doesn't suggest that they are the type who would sneer at the size of your donation; so your donating a chicken or two would make them as happy as your donating a cow.

Vote winner

As a disillusioned voter, I wonder whether it would be ethical, or even legal, to auction my vote on eBay? Is this any worse than not voting at all?

Imagine if everyone were as apathetic as you. Nobody would vote and nobody would get elected to Parliament, and we'd have to hire a private company to run the country. Maybe this management company could be floated on the stock market so that the public could buy and sell shares in the business, with the share price reflecting how much confidence the public had in how well the company was doing its job.

Actually, put like that, it doesn't sound like such a bad idea. Britain's new boss could even raise funds for more schools and hospitals by getting Coca-Cola to sponsor the country ('Britain – it's the real thing!'), and hiring out Oxfordshire for corporate events.

Ethics aside, even if you wanted to hawk your vote, you couldn't. The Electoral Commission says that it is unlawful to buy or sell a vote, under the Representation of the People Act. Then again, catching you committing such a crime might be tricky because, in a way, we all sell our vote to some sweet-talking politician who then doesn't even stay for breakfast the morning after, but simply leaves a note saying: 'Thanks. Let's do that again in five years.'

You should use your vote. Why? Because it is sobering to visit your local polling station and see the others who will be voting. With many of them, you share nothing beyond the right to trial by jury. Are they likely to be thinking what you're thinking? Do you want them to have a more influential say in local or national affairs than you?

Look, nobody's saying that if you vote, you're going to get a great MP. But you might get a less bad one.

Bond adventure

? *My nine-year-old son, who has been given Premium Bonds by a generous uncle, has just won £50 and is delighted that he has money to buy toys and games. But I worry about what would happen were he to win the £1 million prize. Would it be ethical for me to use such a win to benefit us both now – by moving to a better house, say, or giving up my job so that I could be with him more?*

Does it really worry you what to do, were your son to win £1 million with his Premium Bonds? You might as well worry about aliens materialising in your kitchen, cooking themselves some Pot Noodles, catching an episode of *Jerry Springer* on TV and wondering, 'How come someone from a planet peopled by such evidently advanced life forms has never managed to travel to our galaxy?' Have you ever known anyone who has won £1 million on Premium Bonds?

When the Premium Bond statisticians sit down to work out how long to make the odds of winning the jackpot, they imagine the most unlikely turn of events – a llama winning the Grand National; or Donald Rumsfeld quitting politics to become a stand-up comic; something like that – and then they make the odds four zillion times less likely than that.

But were your son to win that £1 million prize, it would be up to him what he did with it. You might persuade him that moving to a nicer house (bought in his name) would not only make life sweeter, but would also make a sturdy investment. But as for giving up your job, that's quite an intangible investment for a young boy. When Oscar Wilde said that children begin by loving their parents, then they judge them and that rarely, if ever, do they forgive them, he wasn't even talking about £1 million being part of the emotional equation.

Taxing times

My accountant has found that HM Revenue and Customs has made an error in my favour and asks permission to alert them. I say that he is employed by me, so I don't see why I should pay him £200 an hour to engage in a lengthy correspondence that will result in my paying more tax. I think it's for the Revenue to put its own house in order. Am I morally and legally right?

Well, if the folk at HM Revenue & Customs don't know that you owe them tax, how are they going to spot you now among the millions of tax returns they're leafing through at this, their busiest time of the year – eh, Mr Jeremy Tollmarch-Fanshawe, of 162 Wivvenhill Mansions, Bildenborough, South Yorkshire YP4 2XR? (Hah hah hah! Just my little joke, Mr Taxman! Jeremy doesn't really live at 162 Wivvenhill Mansions. He lives at no 178.)

An 'error in your favour' is the mirage of the tax world. It just doesn't exist in real life. It's like the empty parking bay you spot in the distance in Knightsbridge on the Saturday before Christmas, only to realise, once you get close to it, that it's for use only by doctors.

Not mentioning its error to the tax office is like painting over a damp patch in your house. It might camouflage things for a while. A year. Maybe longer. But you always know that it's lurking just under the surface. And sooner or later, someone in HM Revenue and Customs turns his gaze to it and shrieks: 'Whoah! See that spot of damp? Lucky we spotted it before it got really bad.'

You are morally and legally on thin ice. But it's academic: they'll notice soon enough. Unless the Revenue genuinely has made an error in your favour. In which case, go shopping in Knightsbridge around Christmas: you're certain to find a free parking space.

An accident waiting to happen

My boyfriend's stepsister is planning a gloss-paint 'accident' on their sitting room, hall and stair carpet, because they could never afford to replace so large an area of carpet themselves. I am fuming, because I think that, apart from being illegal, it's unfair that the majority of us have to pay higher premiums to cover such claims. Should I let it go?

Many people find the whole idea of insurance suspicious; especially life insurance, in which the insurer pays out only when you are no longer around for the money to be of any use to you. So they decide to re-interpret insurance premiums as not so much a means of financial protection but more as a kind of saving scheme. With an occasional inventive claim, the scheme can recoup all that you pour into it over the months; with the bonus that every now and then it pays out a jackpot big enough to recarpet your entire house after a gloss-paint 'accident'.

To these people, the policy renewal date serves as a deadline for earning back their annual premium. Every so often they file a claim big enough to lift them firmly into the black. Insurance companies respond by pushing up the premiums for everyone; or they charge you less each year, providing that you never claim (a trick Houdini would envy). The insurer's 'no claims bonus' is like a £50-a-head restaurant agreeing to charge you only £30 a head, providing you don't stay and eat.

But even if your boyfriend's stepsister believes that insurers behave sharply, it is no reason to defraud them. If she thinks she's being gouged, she could always skip having any home insurance at all, confining herself instead to insuring herself against ever needing insurance.

House work

? *I thought that a house for sale that I viewed was OK, but overpriced. I work in a solicitor's office and later, while handling a client's file, I recognised the address as that of the house I'd viewed. On reading the man's divorce notes I discovered that he thinks the house is not worth the asking price and would accept £10,000 less. May I act on my inside knowledge?*

Better to see a house you consider overpriced and later discover that the owner also thinks that the price is a bit full, and would be prepared to consider offers, than to view a house you consider a bargain for which you'd happily pay more only to learn that the owner thinks the property's a bit of a dog and would be happy to be shot of it at almost any price.

The property market is driven by a weird psychology. That's why Freud devoted his energy to trying to fathom simple mysteries – such as why grown men want to dress in black latex and be lashed by a woman the size of a telephone kiosk dressed in a nurse's outfit that wouldn't fit even Kate Moss – rather than trying to unravel the subconscious minds of housebuyers.

A house-hunter will decide that he or she hates a property; until he hears that it's going to sealed bids. Then he's mad keen for it. When the market is flat, nobody wants to pay the £500,000 asking price for a house, even if they love it, because they don't want to be taken for a schmuck. Three months later, when the market is in its latest frenzy, the same person will pay £550,000 for that property because the vendor could be asking

£600,000 next week. Suddenly it's a bargain!

It is unethical to profit from inside information. You must still come clean. If the vendor thinks you're chiselling him, he can always hold out for a better offer from elsewhere.

Losing your shirt

> *I have seen the most gorgeous shirt for £275. I can afford it, but still have a sense of the value of money. I would spend £275 on a coat, but not on any other item of clothing. Is this distinction fundamentally flawed? I would wear the coat more, and it's a larger garment, but so what?*

Really? £275? I can't recall having ever seen a shirt for £275, whether Prada, Brioni, Charvet or Jermyn Street. Even if you can afford it, do you have reliable enough taste to buy it?

One reason that suits have lasted longer in Britain than elsewhere is that British men struggle to put together an outfit where the trousers don't match the jacket. Casual dress for many men is still shorts and T-shirts that they've owned since they were nineteen (they're now forty-two), worn regardless of whether the strange collage of colours makes everyone else's eyes bleed. A casually dressed British male can step outdoors looking like a human kaleidoscope. Men who think their car stereo is obsolete after nine months remain convinced that their clothes have been constantly in fashion since 1978.

But let's say you pass the taste test: who are you buying the shirt for? If it's to attract women, then if you look anything like Brad Pitt or Johnny Depp you needn't bother going so far. A £60 shirt will suffice. When a face like Pitt's or Depp's is peeping out over the shirt collar, women don't spend a lot of time inspecting the quality of the needlework below.

Just remember: there's a difference between liking nice clothes and being interested in them. For men, the former is quite acceptable; the latter, a bit suspect. This is how it works: I own a fabulously luxurious shirt; you are a spendthrift; he has more money than taste.

Going to the dogs

Misplacing a £5 note during a night at the dogs, I moaned that it must have slipped from my pocket when I was fumbling with betting slips. A friend later found £5 on the ground – possibly mine; most probably not. She was going to give it to charity but, on hearing of my misfortune, offered it to me. Since I have not profited from this situation, am I morally in the clear?

The arithmetic seems so neat, doesn't it? You lose a £5 note. Your friend later finds £5. You take the £5 from your friend. Your wallet's all square by the end of the evening. It's as if a mysterious and benign force of accountancy has intervened to balance the books (not a real accountant, obviously, because they'd have wanted to see some supporting paperwork for those lost and found fivers: an accountant doesn't like to see a client paying someone even a compliment without getting a receipt).

But maybe the arithmetic was just a little too neat. Merely not profiting from a situation is not all that useful, or reliable, a yardstick for gauging whether or not you are morally 'in the clear'. Say a diner who has forgotten to bring a raincoat on what turns out to be a showery evening grabs yours from the coat rack when leaving a restaurant. Would it leave you morally 'in the clear' if you responded by swiping another hapless diner's raincoat when you leave, on the ground that you are not actually ahead on the deal (and, if anything, possibly much worse off, given many men's taste in raincoats)?

Yours was a convenient solution to an inconvenient misfortune. It happened at a race course, so you might call it luck. Ethically, it was like finding someone else's winning betting slip and cashing it in to compensate for your own losses with the bookies.

Musical drama

> ? *I bought tickets for myself, my brother and our girlfriends for a gig by a favourite band of ours. A week before the show, my brother realised he'd forgotten about it and had booked a holiday. He was unable to sell his tickets. I hurriedly sold them for him and made £30 profit. I gave him what he'd paid me for them, but he says he should also get the profit. I think it is mine.*

It's always heartening, isn't it, to come across two brothers who have such a warm bond that they're happy to instigate a wounding family rift over £30 – presumably not a bankruptcy-threatening sum for people who can afford concert tickets and last-minute holidays? Nothing is likelier to cause awkwardness in a family than money squabbles; apart from incest.

Man has been struggling for centuries to work out how best to divide the profits on a deal – or, at any rate, he's been struggling ever since it became bad form to settle such disputes with shotguns. God invented Chancellors of the Exchequer to try to ease the problem by seizing enough of any profit to make further squabbles over how to split what's left feel almost academic. Man's response was to invent the Cayman Islands and Swiss bank accounts.

By buying the tickets, and later reselling your brother's pair, you provided the labour that generated the £30 profit. On the other hand, your brother provided the capital that was invested to harvest that return. But the profit here was an unexpected windfall. Your brother would probably have been happy just to break even. My hunch would be to split the £30. But the most ethical, decent course of action must be more complicated than that, because you would have thought of something so obvious yourselves, wouldn't you?

cat's mess

?   *When a neighbour's cat entered my house to stop my two cats defending their territory, I closed the kitchen doors until I could ensure the visiting cat's safe exit. The interloper began to climb curtains, detaching the curtain pole from the wall and damaging my newly painted kitchen walls. Should I seek compensation from the owners of the cat?*

What possesses a cat to climb up your curtains? Who can say? You can never really tell what's going on in a cat's head. Sometimes, it can look as if a cat has three heads, because it often seems to be thinking three different things simultaneously: hence the cat-owner's call-sign, 'Here, kitty, kitty, kitty'.

You acted thoughtfully because you were raised to believe that virtue is its own reward. Hah, hah, hah! You were also brought up to believe in Father Christmas and the tooth fairy, but you don't still believe in those, do you?

What you did was perform an act of kindness which, had things turned out well, nobody would have known about but you. Your reward would have been not applause or praise but knowing that you had acted considerately and that you would have felt wretched had you acted otherwise. When you act virtuously (and this may not seem fair but, then, life isn't fair, otherwise Arthur Mullard wouldn't have been born looking the way he did), the consequences become your burden. If you rush into traffic to save a child from the path of a speeding car and that child is saved, but you are injured, you cannot seek compensation from the child or its parents.

You could always mention the cat episode to your neighbour, who may get the hint and find a way of rewarding you. Or not. Cat-owners can be as mysterious as their cats.

Building resentment

A builder has offered to do work on my house without applying VAT. He expects me to be delighted, but I'm embarrassed. I don't want to cheat, though if I stand firm the builder will have to declare the job and pay tax on it. If that means he no longer wants the job I don't care. But people tell me I'm being too scrupulous and that this is 'the way things are done'.

How about if you agree to this builder's scheme to outman-oeuvre the taxman (through the builder sparing you the VAT on the work, in return for his not having to declare his income) by adding a delicious additional layer of deception? Tell the builder that to maximise the financial drain on the nation you will pay him in counterfeit banknotes. He'll probably be delighted at your mischievous ingenuity. What do you reckon?

Just because this is 'the way things are done' doesn't make this way right, honourable, or legal. The reason people turn a blind eye to the 'the way things are done', and may even succumb to doing things that way themselves, is because they are greedy, not because such behaviour is ethically neutral. Nobody is thrilled about paying taxes, but the way to change tax rates is through the ballot box, not by unilaterally granting yourself tax-haven status.

By evading VAT and income tax, not only do you deprive the Treasury of cash it needs to build hospitals and schools, you risk swelling the tax burden on your fellow citizens. The people advising you may not grasp that if we all did things 'the way things are done' we would have no hospitals for our sick, our children would be untaught and there'd be so few police we'd have to hire Dick Cheney and his shotgun to defend our homes from attack by Republican lawyers.

Give me credit

> *While visiting my daughter abroad, I had to extend my stay and buy a new return ticket. My credit-card statements do not yet show the $450 charge for this fare. Is it incumbent on me to inform the overseas agent of this? And since the pound has weakened against the dollar, is the agent liable for the extra, in sterling, that the ticket would now cost me?*

You can urge the travel agent to collect his fees promptly; or you can stay silent and gamble that the debit for the fare may never show up on your credit-card statement. What you cannot do is play for a gamble, and later beg to be treated on the same terms as you would have enjoyed had you been honest enough to alert the travel agent to his oversight straight away. If that's how gambling worked, casinos would soon go out of business, and candidates more implausible even than Arnold

Schwarzenegger would try their luck running for serious political office.

It's possible that your card company is so focused on trying to lure new customers with offers of interest-free credit that it's too busy to collect cash from existing cardholders. By the time it remembers, the unpaid debts of these customers will have swollen so dramatically that they will feel impelled to hunt for a new card-issuer that can offer them zero-interest rates on balance transfers. In this way, the same debt keeps circling the financial system until it grows so huge and unrepayable that banks just write it off and start the credit cycle again.

Meanwhile, it is both your financial and moral duty to pay for your ticket. Your agent may consider shouldering your sterling losses if you pay him the interest you've been earning on his uncollected $450.

Hit and run

? *A parking meter swallowed my money without issuing a ticket, despite my banging it several times. While I hunted fruitlessly for a warden, another parker was similarly denied. He punched the machine harder than I had, and £1 coins poured out. 'Let's just split it,' he said. Was I justified in seeing this as compensation for the angst I had suffered?*

It's heartening to hear that the ancient, all-purpose remedy of giving a recalcitrant piece of technology a good slapping is still going strong. Remember when your dad would thump the side of the TV whenever the picture went haywire?

That was in a gentler age, before the era when the instruction manual for even a torch now runs to sixty pages of explanation of how to insert the batteries, followed by a further ten pages of litigation-avoiding safety advice ('This is not a foodstuff: do not eat . . . Not suitable for use as a hammer . . . Do not swallow the batteries . . . This torch cannot shine any light on the mystery of Joss Stone's popularity').

If only Microsoft could invent software that responded to the slaps aimed at their computers by frustrated users on being told that, as a result of their having just performed 'an illegal operation', their computer will be spending the next twenty minutes in the electronic version of a sulk. And think how much more smoothly government would run if you could just thump Geoff Hoon on the side of the head to reset him each time he malfunctioned.

Though your fury may be justified, you have no moral right to exact compensation unilaterally. The fact that those who enforce parking regulations occasionally act with rough justice is no reason for you to sink to their level.

Stamp duty

When letters were delivered with the stamps uncancelled, I used to cut them off and re-use them. But now I think that that was dishonest, so I ignore the temptation. After all, the Royal Mail has completed its obligation of posting that letter to me, so why shouldn't it be paid?

People are understandably amazed that an envelope, marked only with the name and address of a friend, can travel from their local post box in West London across many hundreds of miles to the other side of the country, where it is deposited gently by a postman through a letterbox – amazed because the friend to whom the letter was addressed also lives in West London.

This might explain your gratitude when a letter arrives safely at its destination, without having been mis-delivered, or dumped over a hedge by a postman keen to get home early, or roughly handled by a postal worker who thought that the sticker marked 'Fragile' simply meant that the parcel should on no account be drop-kicked across the sorting office, but that a gentle toss to a colleague twenty yards away wouldn't do the package's contents any lasting harm.

When you have a competent postlady, as I currently have, the mail system is a marvel of efficiency, and not especially expensive for all that is involved. So you are right to think it unethical to re-use an uncancelled stamp, the Royal Mail having met its part of the bargain.

It is no different from not alerting a shopkeeper to the fact that he has handed you too much change. The Royal Mail may have decided it was more important to expedite the delivery of mail than to risk any delay by confirming that each stamp had been rendered unusable. It seems churlish to profit from a situation that may have arisen as a result of the firm's diligence.

Sweet charity

I have found that one way of paying off my large overdraft is to buy designer labels from local charity shops, then resell them on eBay for a profit. But I feel guilty that the charity shops are not getting as much as they could for these clothes. Should I feel guilty?

Charity shops are not greenhorns. Some now price designer clothes so extravagantly that you might find the same items, unworn, more cheaply in the designer's own shop in the sales. Oxfam has a menswear shop in the West End of London to tap into shoppers' thirst for clothes with designer labels, but not quite designer price tags. Your eBay customers seek the same thing.

The marketplace is a pretty efficient regulator of how much something will fetch. Goods tend to be priced at just about the level that buyers will stomach paying for them; whether the item is a breath mint or a Bentley. Charity shops charge a price that they think will get frocks off their rails quickly, and boost cash flow, without short-changing their charity. That's how the retail chain works: leave a cut for the next guy.

If you wanted to drive to Norfolk to buy carrots directly from a farmer and resell them door to door, thereby avoiding your local grocer's mark-up, nobody's stopping you. That's assuming that they even grow carrots in Norfolk: most of us have never tried to find out. We sub-contract our grocer to buy our carrots for us.

Soon enough the gap between what you pay in charity shops and what you sell for on eBay will narrow as others pile in to exploit the same arbitrage margin as you. Charity shops will respond to increased demand for their goods by tweaking their prices. Meanwhile, there is nothing to stop you making a donation to the charity to assuage any guilt you might feel.

Off your trolley

> *If a supermarket checkout operator fails to scan an item, what would your position be if you were stopped at the exit, there being more goods in your trolley than shown on your receipt? Is this accidental advantage*

any different from someone who leaves an item underneath the trolley to avoid paying for it at the till?

It's a question of intention. If you turn sharply on a crowded street and your hand hits a child's face, that's an accident. If you bend down to punch the child, that's assault. If you unwittingly pass someone a foreign coin that you were yourself just handed in a store, your conscience is clear. If you confect a fake British coin and deliberately palm it off in a shop, it's fraud. If you're a famous pop singer and you foist a dreary record on the public, that's a mishap. If you do it again and again, you're Britney Spears.

It's not the ends alone that matter, but also the means to those ends. If Dolly Parton were born with boobs as big as bison, then we might feel pity for her; but since she's chosen to swell them to that size, we deem it purely a matter for her and her structural engineer. Or take Iraq: many now say the streets are no safer, torture no less random, than when Saddam Hussein ruled the country; but George Bush and Tony Blair might at least claim that their moral position is different (more underprepared innocents than knaves, maybe) since they meant well and things just turned sour, whereas for Saddam, terror and torture were express goals.

Accidentally leaving a supermarket with goods you didn't pay for as a result of a checkout operator's error does not make you a thief; any more than a checkout operator who mistakenly scans the same item twice is a racketeer.

Service fault

 I played men's doubles in a 'pay and play' tennis session in which I did not know the other players.

My partner's first serve rocketed into my right temple and smashed my glasses. When I asked for half the £96 cost of new frames, he paid reluctantly, saying that it was an accident. But had he driven into my car by accident he would have been liable for the lot, wouldn't he?

Humans are inconsistent, often behaving in very different ways in quite similar circumstances. We tip waiters, but not shop assistants. Britons snort at how Americans could elect someone like George Bush; *twice!* Then we vote in Ken Livingstone as Mayor of London; *twice!* We go to war, which kills people, because we think it the best way to secure peace and save lives. We sip organic coffee while smoking carcinogenic cigarettes. We fly to hot beaches, only to cower under shade-giving parasols. Waiting for a phantom train on a London Underground platform, we listen to station staff delivering a 'service update announcement' when we know that what they will actually mean is a 'non-service update announcement'.

Were your tennis partner to have crashed into you while you and he were both in your cars, then you'd be right: he'd have been liable for compensating you for any dents in your bodywork. On a tennis court, where third-party and comprehensive insurance is not so common as in motoring, we often regard breakages as mishaps: it is courteous to offer compensation, but a sincerely meant apology can soothe just as well. Inconsistent? Yes.

But sport often serves as a litmus test for how people behave in society: when batsmen start suing bowlers who let loose painful bouncers, or umpires who give them out when they weren't, we're all doomed.

Window of opportunity

While I was buying curtains, I discovered just in time that the shop staff were incompetent. Had I not guided them through the measuring, I'd have ended up with curtains the wrong size. Their arithmetic proved to be just as hopeless, and I was charged half what I should have been. Should I have, again, pointed out their mistake? Or, as I did, pay up and make a hasty retreat?

What if your curtain bill had been for £500 and you had accidentally made out your cheque for £5,000? Would you then have applauded the shop's sang-froid in not informing you of your clumsiness, and calmly escorting you off their premises while praying that you would not spot your error before leaving? Now I know that the odds on my getting the correct answer to this question are, theoretically, fifty-fifty, but I'm willing to go mad and bet your answer is: 'No'. Did I win?

You cannot exact your own revenge from an incompetent shopworker any more than you can exact it from someone who steals your bicycle, or spills their coffee over your expensive dress. There are procedures for getting even with people who have irritated or crossed us. Otherwise we'd all still be settling scores by fighting duels at dawn every morning (or at any rate, we'd be fighting duels at least once, if we happened to be useless at handling an épée or a pistol. That would certainly teach us not to make a customer's curtains too short again; only there wouldn't be an 'again' – there being no 'again' for at least one of the participants being the general point of duels).

Some people seem to think that if you're not actually pointing a gun at someone's temple, while wearing a stocking pulled over your head, it's not, technically, stealing. It is. And all for curtains, for heaven's sake! Pull yourself together!

Talking shop

While Christmas shopping in the city centre, my girlfriend began to feel ill. Cutting the trip short, I still had a few hours left on my parking ticket, so I stuck it to the ticket machine for someone else to use. Was I right to help another driver, or wrong to cost the car park owner a lost fee?

It's easy to see why your girlfriend might feel queasy when shopping in a city centre, especially with the arrival of cold weather, because this is the time of year when stores turn on their patented customer-retention devices. I'm talking about those powerful heaters, positioned just inside the shop's doors, which emit a wall of hot air at customers trying to leave the store. It is like a challenge from a medieval fable: 'To leave this store you must first do battle with the wall of heat, leaving you either (a) feeling faint, or (b) with hair more blow-dried than Jon Bon Jovi's.'

Presumably the idea is that you become so hot that the temperature outside the store feels even lower than it is, persuading you to retreat inside the shop to buy more goods. This process continues until you are so laden with carrier bags that you can no longer fit through the shop's front doors; leaving the store no option but to escort you out of the building through a rear exit that is not guarded by a treacherous wall of heat.

By offering the unused portion of your parking ticket to someone else, you might feel your behaviour to have been ethically sound, your having paid for a space for several hours. You were certainly helping out another driver, but not the operator of the car park, which has pitched its fees after calculating parking patterns. If everyone passed on unused hours of their tickets, the operator might simply raise prices to make up the shortfall.

Insurance policy

Three years ago I reached a settlement with an insurance company after negligence by one of its clients. The award included £7,000 for the probable acceleration by five years of osteoarthritis in the neck. A year ago, cancer was diagnosed. The probability now is that death will predate any acceleration. Should I repay the £7,000?

Will you excuse me for a moment while I phone *Guinness World Records* to register the first known instance of someone feeling sorry for an insurance company?

Insurers calculate premiums in such a way as to ensure that they can lose money only if their actuaries are all spending their lunch breaks smoking crack. And just in case an actuary should err in his sums, insurers invented the excess: this is basically the insurance world's version of Tony Soprano warning you to mind your own business, if you know what's good for you. An excess is designed to make you think twice about filing a claim. The higher the excess you agree to on your policy, the lower the premium, a tantalising give-and-take formula that results in your being able to insure a new Bentley for just £1.79 a year, providing you're willing to foot the first £270,000 of any claim.

Reimbursing the insurer might seem noble. But repaying the £7,000 is neither morally merited nor wise. The insurance company does not feel cheated because, as I have outlined, it is mathematically difficult to outmanoeuvre an insurer. And with the advances in cancer treatment, there is every reason to hope that you will live long enough to deserve the payout. If you feel you cannot enjoy the cash, why not donate it to a worthier cause than an insurance company?

Dropping in on the neighbours

My new computer automatically picks up wireless networks to gain access to the internet; including that belonging to a neighbour. This adds nothing to my neighbour's costs, and I'm not downloading anything (and, so, not using up any potential limits). Is it ethical for me to continue using this?

It's not simply that it is not internet etiquette to piggyback on a neighbour's wireless connection; or that you're depriving your neighbour's broadband provider from earning revenue from you, were you to open your own personal internet account; or that sponging off your neighbour's net connection is similar to making copies of all new CDs that your friends buy without ever returning the favour. It's that records exist in cyberspace of every website visited by you or by your neighbour, and of every e-mail that you or your neighbour sends.

How does the web do this? Only three people in the world know for certain, and it's very likely they live in Bangalore and can be contacted only via a premium-rate telephone line that welcomes you with the traditional computer helpline greeting of 'You are held in a queue and will be answered shortly. Your position in the queue is number . . . 4,972. At the current call-charge rate, you might find it cheaper to purchase a new computer than to keep holding.'

So, if someone using that shared internet connection visits a dodgy website, the authorities might be able to trace it back and expose you. It will be embarrassing enough for your neighbour to realise that you now know that he visits those porn sites where you have to swivel your head sideways even to discern who is doing what to whom. But how much more embarrassing will it be if your neighbour finds out that you're a regular visitor to Mick Hucknall's fan site?

Forging ahead

Having been given £50 in a cashback transaction at a supermarket, I was annoyed later to be told, when paying my bill at a café, that a £20 note I had received from the supermarket till was a forgery. Knowingly passing counterfeit money is a serious offence. But is spending the forged £20 at the same supermarket which gave it to me ethically acceptable in the circumstances?

Being stuck with a counterfeit banknote is the financial equivalent of being the last person standing in musical chairs. How can it be moral for you to pass on the forged £20 note, whether or not you yourself were originally a victim?

As for the Bank of England, its chief cashier promises 'to pay the bearer on demand the sum of Twenty Pounds'. He doesn't promise 'to pay the bearer on demand the sum of Twenty Pounds just because a note happens to look quite like genuine Bank of England currency'.

Can you pass it back to the supermarket that passed it to you? Tempting, certainly. But ethical? No. There may appear to be no difference between spending a counterfeit banknote that you don't know was forged and spending one that you know to be a fake, but it is very different in moral terms. In the first, the music is still playing as the forged note circulates around the economy. In the second, you are deliberately seeking to deceive. That you were taken for a ride doesn't make it morally acceptable to make a patsy out of the next man.

It's similar to gossip: you may pass on a salaciously incriminating story as long as you believe it to be true. Once you know it to be a groundless calumny, you may not repeat it. That's why gossips never seek that final extra telltale fact that might ruin a good story.

Making a play for it

I go to the theatre quite often and always buy the cheapest seats. When the interval comes, it is frequently clear that there are more expensive seats that are empty. It seems a waste, so I like to move to them for the second half. Is this acceptable?

By moving to an empty seat you are not hurting anyone: the theatre is making no more and no less money than it would have taken at the box office when the curtain rose, and you are enjoying a better view. There would seem to be an evident net gain, especially since, by your waiting until the interval, it is unlikely that you will be disturbing anyone as a result of the seat's owner turning up and forcing you to shuffle back to your proper seat mid-soliloquy.

On the other hand, what if everyone who went to the theatre behaved as you do? Fewer theatregoers would buy the expensive tickets, perhaps gambling on there always being a good chance of moving, as soon as the house lights had dimmed, to a pricier seat nearer the stage.

So what's to stop them? The same thing that stops shoppers waiting for the January sales for the chance to buy at half-price a suit or sofa they covet: by sale time that suit or sofa may have been sold. Seat-switchers see their bonus as a windfall, rather than the reward for a Machiavellian seat-stealing strategy. At the same time, if the trend were so big that theatregoers who bought the posh seats felt like patsies and stopped going, all ticket prices would rise and playgoers would not have a chance to buy cheap seats at all.

The surest solution would be for theatres to put on better shows. That way there'd be no empty seats in the house for seat-swappers to colonise. So no more Jeffrey Archer plays, then.

Net gain

Seeking to buy a twenty-minute, £1 ticket at an internet café, I was told they had sold out. As I turned to leave, the kind person behind the counter offered me a sixty-minute, £3 internet ticket for £1. Is it morally wrong to use all sixty minutes, or should I use only the twenty minutes I have paid for?

You should use only the twenty minutes – not because that's all you've paid for, but because if you had needed to spend an hour on the net you'd have paid to do so. Therefore clicking away for those extra 'free' forty minutes is just stealing a piece of your life, probably for little reward.

Internet time is like dog years: for every hour you think you have spent surfing, you've actually spent seven. In the internet world there are only six degrees of separation – or hypertext clicks – from checking the source of the Nile to visiting the box office for Celine Dion's cabaret show at Caesars Palace, via a Turkish recipe for baked chicken. You might log on to inquire if Dulux has launched a new shade of white called 'Michael

Jackson's Face' and by the time you log off you find that your wife has retired and your children have grown up and left home; which is creepy because when you sat down you didn't even *have* children.

The way telephone-line time is charged, the café will probably not be out of pocket if you surf for longer than the time you paid for; and it is earning £1 it might not otherwise have earned. To leave after twenty minutes, though, would show good manners and would indicate to the person behind the counter that their goodwill had not been abused.

Trolley-to-car Service

? *As we were unloading heavy bags of topsoil from a trolley in a garden-centre car park, the wind caught the loaded trolley and sent it careering down a slope and into a parked car, causing a noticeable two-inch dent in the wing. We apologised to the owner. Should we also have offered money towards a repair?*

Your mishap is one more instance of how townies' obsession with gardening spells problems for all. Aren't there enough public parks to satisfy city-dwellers eager for an occasional change of scenery? Why do you need your own personal Kew Gardens at the back of your house, any more than you need your own personal Selfridges department store or your own personal football stadium?

Now there is a fresh mania among townsfolk: getting hold of an allotment. An allotment is the formal horticultural unit of measurement denoting 'an area of land capable of producing more courgettes than anyone could conceivably consume, even if they were afflicted by a rare condition that would result in their dying if they failed to eat six courgettes at every meal'.

Exactly why should anyone in a city ever need 'heavy bags of topsoil'? But having made this purchasing error, you compound it by citing the wind's part in your accident, as if maybe the whole thing could be attributed to an act of God. When you have a trolley, you are its guardian, in the same way as you are the guardian of your wayward child. Leaving your trolley at the top of a slope, and at the whim of the wind, is an act not of God but of carelessness. You should certainly have offered money towards a repair. I hope only that you did not offer to appease the injured car-owner with a crate of courgettes, or they would have been within their moral rights to tell you not just how to stuff them, but where.

Lucky gym

> **?** At my gym, I often find a £1 coin left in a locker. The first time this happened, I gleefully kept it, as I had recently lost a £1 coin in the same circumstances. But now that my account is straight, what should I do with the coins I find? I doubt that anyone ever goes back to lost property to reclaim their missing money. Should I give the money to charity?

That depends on how much you have come to see your role in life as taking the law into your own hands. You have already squared your conscience by assuring yourself that you were morally entitled to keep a £1 coin that a fellow gym-user had left behind in a locker, because you had lost £1 in identical circumstances ('in identical circumstances' here meaning 'as a result of my own forgetfulness'). You have now weighed the evidence in the kangaroo court of your mind and further decided that, should you find more £1 coins in the future, it would be pointless to hand them in to the gym's reception because their owners probably wouldn't bother to reclaim them; so you might as well take the decision on how best this money might be used.

Why stop there? If you catch burglars in your house, why not act on your hunch that, even if caught by the police, the robbers might well wriggle out of a prison term on some technicality, in which case you might as well exact your own justice now with a baseball bat while you can?

But why stop there, either? Since you possess such a polished instinct for knowing what's best for others, and for the world in general, why not exercise this talent more widely? How about entering music stores and, as an act of benevolence, scratching all of James Blunt's CDs to spare innocent people the risk of buying them, with all the resulting aural distress?

Dress code

After buying a dress, I decided it didn't really suit, so returned it. Not having the receipt, I was entitled only to credit vouchers. I used £60 on a top, but I still have £20 in vouchers that I am unlikely to use. Is it wrong to return the top (with receipt) for a full cash refund at another branch, then buy it back later using the vouchers?

Vouchers are the 'Gotcha!' of the retailing world. When you return an item to a shop and it gives you vouchers instead of cash in exchange, it is basically telling you: 'You spent your money in our store and we're damned if we're now going to let you harm our profits by allowing you to spend it anywhere else.

So here's a voucher instead. It's like regular money in that if this shop ever grows so big that it becomes an independent nation state, then this voucher will be no different from, say, a £20 note in the UK, and you'll be able to spend it in any shop or restaurant. Until such time, though, you can spend it only here, with us. Ha ha ha!'

There are occasionally good reasons for a shop to issue vouchers: for instance, if a sale is on and you don't have a receipt to prove that you bought the returned goods at full price. Otherwise, giving out vouchers indicates a shop's lack of confidence in its products. It betrays a fear that, with cash in your hand, you'll flee and never trouble its tills again.

Actually, shops that run a generous returns policy benefit from shoppers making dubious impulse buys, knowing that they'll be able to return them, but generally they can't be fagged to trek back to the store even if, once they've got it home, they realise they don't actually need a TV screen the size of Idaho. As long as you genuinely just lost your receipt, go ahead.

Royalty Statement

I wrote a book that proved to be rather successful. I received daily fan mail from friends and strangers, telling me how much they loved it, and how many friends they had lent it to. Am I being churlish in feeling that these people behaved unethically in depriving me of royalties by lending their single copy to five or six friends, instead of encouraging them to buy their own?

First off, don't be disheartened about feeling cheesed off. Authors are rarely happy. And because they're unhappy they may go out of their way to make others unhappy, too. Often the easiest way they can think of to do this is by writing yet more books. This may only make matters worse for the author. A reader who buys a dismal novel has wasted only £7.99. The author of that novel has wasted a year; and would probably have earned more by working as the junior assistant his publishing company hires to make bonfires of all unsolicited manuscripts.

Now, it's not clear whether you consider your book to have been successful as a result of its sales, or on account of your fan mail. If the former, it's possible that some of these sales were fostered by the actions of your friends in distributing their copies to others. If it is the latter yardstick – namely, adulation – that you are using to gauge your book's success, it will, if genuine, in turn spawn sales. Not everyone who reads a borrowed copy of your book will buy their own volume; but some will. Others, if they enjoyed it, will remember it when seeking a present for someone.

Lent copies of books are the literary equivalent of those samples they hand you to taste in supermarkets: you may not be looking for salami on this shopping trip, but you might remember that sample you tasted when you next are.

Not present

I enclosed a gift card for £20 in the envelope of a birthday card I sent to the young son of a good friend of mine. Apparently he received the birthday card but not the gift card. Maybe the envelope was tampered with in the post, or the boy threw the envelope away before thoroughly checking it. Do I have a moral obligation to replace the £20?

Who knows what might have happened to the £20 gift card? Maybe the boy noticed that there was something else in the envelope but binned it, thinking that it must be more of that junk mail that now swells every arriving envelope, from magazine subscription to gas bill.

Or maybe he assumed that there was unlikely to be anything in the envelope more valuable than the card itself, what with birthday cards now costing roughly the same as a paperback: Joseph Heller could have made as much in royalties turning the pithy paradox of *Catch-22* into a greeting for a Hallmark card (find it in the *To A Reluctant Soldier* section) without the effort of writing those extra 200,000 words. Maybe the boy is just a bit clumsy. Or the money may have been hijacked by that famous magician who intercepts cash destined for you and helps himself to a slice – a magician sometimes known as the Chancellor of the Exchequer.

But does your obligation end the minute you've posted the envelope? That depends. What was your aim in sending the £20? Was it to give the birthday boy £20 to spend on something that would please him? Or was it solely to make you £20 poorer? If the latter, then you need lose no more sleep over the missing money. But if it was the former, then you do have an obligation to replace the £20: that this leaves you £40 poorer overall is immaterial.

Tipping point

I invited a friend to share a holiday I won. Everything was paid for – flights, hotels, entertainment – except meals. But in restaurants, while agreeing to split the cost of food, my friend refused to contribute towards a tip, saying that she didn't believe in tipping. Having invited her on the trip, was I wrong to expect her to abide by my moral code regarding tipping?

You cannot cajole someone into sharing your moral outlook on life (or make them feel guilty for not sharing your moral values) simply by engineering a situation in which they might feel themselves to be in your debt. Otherwise politicians would be vulnerable to being in the pocket of every favour-seeking corporation, lobby group or peerage-hunting toady who lavished them with cash, anonymous loans, holiday villas, match tickets and even hookers, and can you really imagine any self-respecting politician being bought that cheaply? Certainly not! You'd probably have to throw in the regular use of a private jet as well.

But you *can* expect a friend to chip in towards restaurant tips because it's the decent thing to do; especially when waiters in many countries rely on tips, work hard to earn them, and will often chase you back to your hotel with a cleaver if you fail to leave a decent one. You may also expect a friend who has been given so generous a treat as an all-expenses-paid holiday to behave in a way that makes her host feel that she chose the right vacation companion. In such circumstances, a polite guest might even go out of their way to pick up rather more than their fair share of restaurant bills, by way of thanks for the invitation.

Refusing to tip is not taking a moral stand, it's ducking for cheapskates.

check in

> **?** *We changed our mortgage lender to get a better rate. The cheque for £400 that we gave the new lender to cover the cost of the transfer has not been cashed. Our mortgage adviser thinks that the mortgage company has forgotten to cash the cheque. We are nearing the end of the six-month validity period for the cheque and were wondering: can we now call the money our own?*

You can call the money Suzy Creamcheese if you like, but it still wouldn't belong to you. Sooner or later the mortgage company will notice that its books aren't balanced. Money lenders, along with banks and accountants, spend a lot of time ensuring that their books are balanced, a process that involves the use of large, finely calibrated weighing scales (when lawyers aren't using the scales to weigh justice: the advent of electronic weighing machines has improved accuracy in accountancy and the law, but has robbed both professions of some of their romance).

When your account was overdrawn, banks used to write to draw your attention to this fact so that 'any error, whether on your part or ours, can be rectified'. And guess what? The error always turned out to be on your part, even when you felt certain that it wasn't and had dialled your bank, ready to be indignant at its impudence. That practice has waned, because now, by the time you've waited twenty-seven minutes to speak to a human at your bank's call centre in Jakarta, you've lost not only the passion necessary for indignation, you've even lost any lingering desire to breathe.

The cheque's six-month validity period is a safety measure, not a statute of limitations on your debts. Sooner or later the discrepancy will show up, and then you'll feel a little tawdry for having tried to keep it a secret.

Card Sharp

> *I apply for credit cards just to get the 'free gift'.*
> *Card arrives, I use it once, gift follows, then I pay off and cancel the card. So far I have collected a set of luggage, two watches, a camera and an alarm clock that tells me the time all over the world, if only I could get it working. Is this immoral?*

The card company may not have your long-term business, but at least it has your name, address, and – because you settled your debt promptly – evidence that you are creditworthy. It could now make money by hawking your name to book clubs, cruise operators, shirt-sellers, insurance companies, and domestic energy-suppliers ('Don't let your present supplier scare you silly with stories about your old boiler breaking down in mid-winter! Switch, and let us be the ones to scare you silly instead!').

These outfits will, in turn, sell your name in their own mailing lists to other businesses; which will do the same. It's the direct-mail version of pyramid-selling. Your name travels further and further afield until one day a letter arrives from a supermarket in Nairobi offering you a 25 per cent discount and free home delivery, and you wonder how they got your address. Now you know how.

Is that worth a free suitcase that will tumble from the airport carousel on its first outing with its zip already broken in transit, embarrassing you by revealing to all your fellow passengers that you own red nylon underwear and – oh, the shame! – a Dan Brown novel?

You are not behaving immorally. The card issuers know that many of the customers they entice will not be long-term clients. What hurts them is having to acknowledge that they have built a client base full of the sort of people who want to own cheap luggage and tacky watches.

Playing the game

My local pub's table-football machine charges £1 a game. Since the tables have low running costs, this seems extortionate. Fortunately, I recently returned from a trip to Swaziland with a stash of one-lilangeni coins. One lilangeni is worth 9p, but the coins are the exact same shape and size as our £1 coins, and work just fine. How evil am I being?

It can be very morally disorientating, can't it, when something is the exact shape and size of something else? Take George Galloway: he is the exact shape and size of an elected Member of Parliament, whereas it turns out that he is, in fact, an embarrassment. Or you might happen to notice something that's the exact shape and size of Michael Moore, but on closer inspection it turns out to be Jennifer Lopez's backside. The evidence submitted to the jury in OJ Simpson's trial appeared to be the exact shape and size of a guilty verdict, but it turned out that Simpson was innocent.

A one-lilangeni coin might be the exact shape and size of a

£1 coin, but it isn't a £1 coin, is it? You have no more right to decide how much is a just price for a game of table football at your local pub than you have a right unilaterally to decide what is a just price to pay for a pint of the pub's beer. Many things have very low running costs once they have been installed (telephone cables; motorways; Channel 4 editors who keep recommissioning *Big Brother*), but the charge for using these goods or services is like an extended payment-by-instalments plan.

Evil? You're not being evil, exactly. But unethical, certainly. And if you persist, you could experience something that is the exact same shape and size as having your collar felt.

Photo finish

I damaged my camera on holiday. My local photography shop quoted me £210 for a new lens, which my insurance company agreed to reimburse, after deducting £75 for the excess. But when I went back to buy the lens, it was no longer being made. So I bought a similar, if not better, ex-display lens for £135. Should I declare the £75 difference to my insurance company?

It's hard to feel too sorry for insurance companies, especially when you see the dismal TV commercials that they inflict on us. I'm thinking particularly of those commercials in which apparently normal adults are reduced to piles of quivering orgasmic jelly by – what? What? By being invited to go yachting with George Clooney? By being begged to spend a weekend in bed with Monica Bellucci? No, by receiving an insurance quotation over the phone. Why would any company choose to insure someone who behaved so disturbingly, indemnifying them for any damage they caused when in control of a fast-moving car?

Your insurer agreed to reimburse you for what you had lost: a particular camera lens that would have cost you £210 to replace. You fully intended to buy that lens, had it still been on sale. That you bought a cheaper replacement leaves your insurer no worse off. You insured a particular risk. Had you insured a pricey designer outfit and decided, after it had been accidentally ruined, that you would make do with a replacement from a charity shop, you are not defrauding the insurance company, unless you deliberately damaged the outfit. You paid an insurance premium for a pricey outfit, not a charity-shop replacement. You are entitled to keep the notional £75; so long as you don't now quiver like a crazed person at your good fortune.

Price-fixing

? *How should one deal with the perennial problem of people who give Christmas presents but insist on leaving the price on the gift? The price is always displayed in a prominent position, evidently deliberately. I am all for returning the price tags with my thank-you letters, but perhaps a more subtle approach is required. How do I make the offenders feel contrite?*

Append extravagantly inflated fake price labels to your own gifts to all those price-tag fetishists so that (a) there is no chance of your being outspent, and (b) the recipient can't fail to get the hint. Or, try including one of these messages in your thank-you letter:

1. 'I felt awkward that the present you bought me evidently cost twice as much as the one I bought you. So please find

enclosed, in addition to my thanks, an IOU for £7.50.'

2. 'I bought you an equally expensive present. But as I handed it to Father Christmas to deliver to you, he became the victim of extraordinary rendition by the CIA.'

3. 'Thank you for the carefully chosen present exposing the tawdry commercialism of modern Christmases. It astounded family members and friends that any shop could have the gall to charge £15 for such a shoddily-made object.'

4. 'How very thoughtful of you to leave the price label on your gift. It made it so much easier for our local Oxfam shop to price it.'

5. 'Thank you for the extravagant gift. The last time I received anything that costly, with the store's price label and security tag still attached, it was from Winona Ryder.'

Toy story

My wife bought a toy for our daughter's birthday from a local shop for £10, but later found it being sold for £30 in a supermarket. She proposes returning the toy to the supermarket for a £30 refund and rebuying it from the original shop. She thinks that this is ethically sound. Is it?

With arbitrage skills like that, has your wife considered offering her services to George Soros, or even starting her own hedge fund? I mean, why stick to chiselling meagre profits from brokering toys when she could be moving billions around the world to milk discrepancies in exchange rates and stock prices?

Unless your wife is a trainee economist seeking to prove that a market for any product will always find its own price level – assuming perfect knowledge by all participants in the marketplace, and what economists call *pari passu* (literally, 'bonus AirMiles') – she has no business ricocheting between the toy shop and supermarket like a well-struck snooker ball.

Though it may be true that the toy shop is making extra sales it might not otherwise have made, and is pocketing a profit from each sale with which it is apparently satisfied, the supermarket is not. It is buying its stock retail (from your wife) and selling it retail: result, as Mr Micawber might say, misery. It may be getting the same price for selling each toy, that is £30, but it is making no profit since it has paid your wife £30 for the toy.

So though she might not be harming the toy shop, she is effectively stealing from the supermarket. The supermarket will soon notice that it is selling more of these £30 toys than it is receiving from its warehouse. But it won't be looking for the staff member who deserves the employee-of-the-month award for pulling off this feat. It will be looking for your wife.

Trained to steal

? *A colleague of mine does nothing to discourage his daughter from travelling to college and back every day without buying a ticket for the train, on the basis that it is cheaper to pay the full adult fare on the days a guard is on board. He considers this thrift. But is it?*

Some people have a moral blind spot when it comes to differentiating between committing an offence and not being caught for having committed an offence. So let's say that they drive their car while simultaneously jabbering on their mobile phone: they do not regard what they're doing as an offence if they are not caught by police for doing it. Such people occasionally like to put a metaphysical sheen on their transgression by suggesting, for instance, that it is a prosaic equivalent of the old philosophical conundrum: if a tree falls down in a forest and there is nobody around to hear it, how can one say that it actually made a noise when it crashed to the floor?

In your colleague's case, if his daughter sits on a spare seat on a train that was going to be travelling anyway, who is she hurting? In truth, it is closer to the Bill Clinton philosophy that says: 'So long as nobody has clear proof to contradict me, I am sure in my own mind that I did not have sexual relations with that woman.'

This way of viewing the world means that a burglar is innocent if he hasn't had his collar felt for stealing; an adulterer hasn't strayed so long as his or her spouse hasn't found out about their philandering; and Michael Jackson is a normal-looking man, providing that you don't open your eyes when he's right in front of you. The fact that it is cheaper to pay the adult fare when caught is an act not of thrift but of theft.

Ruffled over raffle

I have a strong moral objection to any form of gambling. Someone who obviously meant well bought me a Lottery ticket for my birthday. Is it more ethical for me to stick to my principles and throw it away without even finding out if it has won, or checking to see if my ticket has won and putting my winnings to good use – by giving them to, for instance, a charity that helps people addicted to gambling?

Already, any gamblers reading this are calculating the odds of which of the two paths you will follow. Gamblers can't help themselves. A gambler can't see two options without forming a hunch about which is the more likely, and then hunting for a sucker to take the other side of the bet. A gambler will take bets on which raindrop will reach the bottom of a windowpane first. A gambler seated on a plane watching the flight attendant pushing the food trolley down the aisle is not wondering whether to have the chicken or the beef (or, like the rest of us, weighing up whether to accept a food tray from the flight attendant on the one hand or, on the other, to just eat our under-seat life vest because it's almost bound to be both tastier and more nutritious). No, he's wondering what odds a fellow economy-class passenger might offer him of one of the choices on the dinner trolley being something outlandish like, say, squid ink risotto.

Throwing the ticket away sounds ethically noble. Then again, if it's a jackpot-winning ticket and you don't claim it, the money might just be siphoned off to fund Britain's Olympics bill. Donating your jackpot prize to a charity that helps gambling addicts might be one way of wrenching the best out of what you regard as a morally awkward predicament. That's assuming you land the jackpot. Are you mad? Have you seen the odds? Only a gambler would believe he had any chance of winning.

6 Friends (or foes?)

'It takes your enemy and your friend, working together, to hurt you to the heart: the one to slander you and the other to get the news to you'

Mark Twain

christmas tide

We have received another avalanche of 'Aren't we brilliant?' Christmas circular letters. They come with an implication that unless I follow a similar lifestyle I'll never be happy, yet show scant regard for recipients who will never have the means to emulate the heroic deeds described within. They are well meant, so is it wrong to feel upset by them?

There is a thin line between keeping friends informed of your family's news and boasting shamelessly about your safari in Kenya, your success on the Cresta Run, your Nobel award and your children's triumphs. No, actually there's a line as wide as the Grand Canyon.

Brevity is a precious talent in writing. Pascal apologised to a friend for having written him a long letter, explaining that he hadn't had time to write a shorter one. Maybe in a few years' time Christmas cards will come in an electronic form where, as with satellite TV channels, you'll be able to press the red button if you want fuller details of what the Wilkinson-Thrupps have been up to over the past year.

Meanwhile, those who send Christmas circulars might

consider enlivening them by penning them as multiple-choice narratives, asking recipients to guess the correct options throughout. An example: 'Dear Sally and Bill, the past year proved to be a great/horrid/erotic one for our brood, bringing a big improvement in Ralph's salary/golf handicap/flatulence, while the children both landed good jobs at Heathrow on time/in a Thai jail. Sam is much happier now that he has graduated/emigrated/changed sex . . .' and so on. A prize to any recipient who picked all the correct options would put some spice back into this annual correspondence; or we might all lose patience/your address/the will to live.

Suddenly everyone's a comedian!

? *An old school friend has become a fairly successful comedian, appearing regularly on TV. I like the guy, but unfortunately I don't find him funny. I haven't seen him for years, but I'm likely to meet him at a forthcoming class reunion. Should I lie to avoid hurting his feelings, or tell the truth (in a constructive way), so that he might improve his act?*

Say that again: you want to give constructive criticism to a stand-up comedian friend so that such impartial advice, friend to friend, might possibly improve his act? Now that's funny! Really, *really* funny. Have you ever thought of doing a little stand-up yourself? I think you ought to consider it. You've certainly got the right sense of humour.

As you evidently know, what a comic most wants, after he's spent months on a new routine, and hours screwing up the courage to deliver it in front of strangers, is a friend selfless enough to give up his time after the performance to explain exactly why all the jokes bombed. The fact that your friend has notched up many TV appearances suggests that somebody must find him amusing. So maybe the problem lies with you rather than with him. Or it could just be that you and your friend have different senses of humour. That happens. I mean, who would have thought the world would find Benny Hill so funny? Or that Russians would find jokes to tell about Stalin (until Stalin had them shot)?

You have neither a moral obligation to find your friend funny, nor a duty to tell him how his jokes stink like dog poop. Comics have a hard enough time as it is, competing for laughs with what emerges from the mouths of politicians, without their friends turning on them.

Animal instincts

My strict vegan values extend to toiletries and cosmetics. For Christmas, one of my oldest friends gave me bath pearls, which contain gelatine and are tested on animals. Yet I want to honour his generosity, as he spent time and money on a gift for me. Should I not use the bath pearls on ethical grounds, or should I use them out of the respect I hold for my friend?

Your vegan values certainly make it tricky for you to use the bath pearls. Some people might argue that since the bath pearls have already been created, it's not as if any animals' lives will be saved by your not using them. But you might as well argue that Sylvester Stallone has already squandered the world's resources to make yet another *Rocky* movie, so you might as well now go and see it – a conundrum to which Bertrand Russell, were he still alive, would have no hesitation in saying, 'No! That would only encourage him to make more *Rocky* movies.' So explaining to your friend why you are so passionate a vegan might educate him as to which presents to buy you in future.

More immediately, though, a present given with no malicious intent does not deserve to be thrown back in your friend's face. There is no law banning you from graciously accepting the bath pearls and then not using them for a year before passing them on to your local charity. I mean, that's exactly what the rest of us non-vegans do with most of our Christmas presents.

It's eating me up

> **?** *As a student, I share a house with two friends. We usually cook together and share most food, apart from a few individual items, such as cereal. We divide up the cost equally three ways, but one of the housemates is petite and generally eats quite a bit less than we other two. Is it wrong that we effectively make her pay for food that we end up eating?*

Living communally is not the same as living communistically. When it comes to sharing bills among housemates, it is not a question of 'to each according to his needs, and from each according to his consumption'. Give-and-take is an understood part of the formula; an area in which a strict ethical interpretation of fairness might be agreeably trumped by the more laissez-faire generosity bred by friendship.

Student life has many joys. But sharing a flat with someone who monitors everyone's milk usage with marker pens to apportion bills with an accuracy measured to seven decimal places is not among them. (Curiously, these are often the flatmates who end up running those giant corporations where it is acceptable to announce that such-and-such a venture was, in hindsight, a strategic error and so, to draw a line under the past, the company will be writing off the £2 billion loss in one clean hit. These companies use the terms 'strategic error' and 'one clean hit' in a way that would get you or me put in Parkhurst for a long time.) Maybe your petite housemate leaves the lights on more than you do; or watches more TV; or, being less insulated with fat, turns the heating up higher in her bedroom.

If your petite housemate really found the house's size-blind accounting that irksome, she would have arranged to share a house with Tom Cruise instead.

Scent packing

> **?** *My close friend of thirty years has started wearing a new perfume that smells exactly like a cheap bathroom air freshener, which I know it certainly is not. My sensitive nose finds this intolerable close at hand. What is the solution?*

Another person's odour sends off powerful signals about them, but as human beings we don't necessarily know how to read all these signals, on account of our being blessed – when such things as intelligence, senses, etc, were being handed out – with big, well-developed brains.

Dogs, on the other hand, don't have big brains. Instead, they have a powerful sense of smell, which keeps them informed of all that they need to know about the world around them: it's the canine world's primitive version of Western Union. This is why dogs are always sniffing things to discover more about their surroundings. If Christopher Columbus had been a dog he'd have made his decision on whether or not to discover America only after sniffing it exhaustively to identify what kind of odour it was giving off. Then he would have weed over it.

Although most human smells don't send out the same instinctive animal signals as dog smells do, they nonetheless send out other coded messages: for instance, your taste in perfume. What is distressing you is that a friend of thirty years' standing could prove to have such trashy taste in cologne. As a friend, you should be sensitive and forgiving. Maybe she herself is being sensitive and is wearing the new scent because it was given to her by her husband and she doesn't wish to hurt his feelings. If so, you could trump his scent gift by buying your friend some Chanel or Guerlain, which she will then feel obliged to wear when in your company.

Altar ego

My best friend has asked me to be his best man. The snag is that he's getting married in a castle at Lake Garda in high summer, and I simply cannot afford to go. I could put the jaunt on a credit card, but for that amount of debt I would rather replace my clapped-out car. Am I being ungrateful, or is it unreasonable of him to expect people to go abroad for his wedding?

It used to be that it was only the bride's parents who ended the wedding day with an overdraft so big that you could actually hear ATM machines sniggering when they dispensed 'outstanding balance' statements.

Now even guests must dig deep for more than just a

present. The expenses start with the stag night. In a quest for novelty, stag nights have broadened their horizons beyond Prague. They now involve trips to places so remote that even David Attenborough has never visited them. The wedding ceremonies are then staged on a Caribbean beach, or at Uluru, or on a float in the midst of the Rio carnival.

It may be that a bride and groom deliberately choose a faraway setting, calculating that the more distant the venue, the fewer guests they'll have to feed; which is OK so long as the guests can choose whether or not to attend. But skipping the ceremony is not an option for the best man (unless he is still detained at the site of the stag night, where he remains lashed to a Bangkok lamppost by a ladyboy who insists that s/he is now legally his 'wife' and is refusing to release him unless it is to sweep her off to her new marital home in Pinner). A thoughtful groom should not put a hard-up best man in so awkward a position, perhaps providing an airline ticket in thanks for his taking on this role.

Ski bum

Before returning a ski jacket I'd borrowed from a friend, I washed it as she had requested. Some dark colours ran on to paler areas, and the jacket, though still wearable, got some slight staining. When I offered to replace her jacket, my friend presented me with a large bill for a new one. Had the roles been reversed, I would never have accepted such money from a friend.

Had the jacket you borrowed not been made of patches of different coloured fabric, your problem would never have arisen. Unfortunately, makers of ski clothes think it is illegal to use only one colour in a jacket. The reason why many people don't take up skiing is not a fear of breaking limbs, but their reluctance to appear in public dressed like a Dulux colour chart.

Some argue that such noisy outfits improve safety by making you stand out on the slopes. Others see such outfits as a prime cause of skiing accidents: you take your eye off the slopes to alert a companion to a nearby skier who is dressed head to toe in a mix of custard yellow and kiwi-fruit green and – wham! – you've slammed into a tree trunk.

People shouldn't lend things if they're going to be distressed if they come back damaged. Equally, people shouldn't borrow things without understanding that they are responsible for remedying any damage that befalls these items while they're in their care. It's not a case of who blinks first, lender or borrower, but of reaching a sensible, hopefully unspoken, compromise. You behaved honourably by offering to replace the jacket. Unless this was an entirely hollow gesture, you cannot now chastise your friend for accepting your offer; however gracious it might have been for her to do so.

Spellbound

Using my recently acquired internet skills to log on to websites of friends and family, I am startled by the spelling mistakes and grammatical errors on these sites and am now full of do-gooding zeal. Shall I tell these people? Or even offer to correct them for a fee?

Being an internet ingénue, you evidently have not realised that people no longer feel bound by formal rules of spelling and grammar when writing e-mails or text messages, the way they might still feel bound were they committing these same thoughts to paper with a pen. Our brains seem to have adapted so skilfully to this new laissez-faire approach that experiments show that as long as the first and last letter of a word are correctly in place, we can generally understand the sense of a message even if the sentence would look like gibberish to a lexicographer ('Idened, our birans seem to hvae apedtad so slkfilluy to tihs new lissaez-friae aorppach taht exrepeinmts...' – you see what I mean?). Think of it as the visual equivalent of listening to Arnold Schwarzenegger speaking English yet being able to grasp what he is trying to say.

Such taking of liberties with the language reminds you of a Lewis Carroll world in which, when Alice complains to Humpty Dumpty that he is misusing words, Humpty Dumpty scornfully replies: 'When I use a word it means just what I choose it to mean – neither more nor less.' So you could certainly offer to correct spelling and grammar on websites that vex you. But don't be surprised if the site owners respond by offering to gvie u a bg salp in yuor fcae.

Sponge bags

We celebrated my husband's fiftieth birthday with a party. We had twenty house guests over the four days; others in nearby B&Bs. One couple asked to camp in the garden and then joined us for every meal but didn't lift a finger to help, or bring a present. He works in the wine trade and drank plenty but brought not a drop. They are not short of money. Do we take it lying down?

Friendships, like marriages, are under constant review. Which is why friends drift apart; and couples divorce. Our circle might include friends who make Eeyore sound as chirpy as Goldie

Hawn, or who have short arms and deep pockets whenever it comes to picking up a tab. But these people have other virtues that eclipse what others may consider unappetising short-comings.

Either you knew already about these friends' freeloading habits, and forgave them, or you are only now learning something about this couple that may colour your view of them; indelibly. What you cannot do, though, is ask them to stump up for their stay. When we invite friends for dinner, we don't expect them to bring gifts to the value of the food and wine we are about to serve them. That would make us as grubby as you now feel your friends to be. Friendship is not like a balance sheet.

One of the pleasures of friendship is watching your friends enjoy your hospitality and enjoying theirs in return. That this couple is 'not short of money' is neither here nor there. Do you expect more from your rich friends? Is it a case of to each friend according to his needs, and from each according to his credit rating? Do you suppose that's the sort of comradeship that Marx and Engels had in mind when framing *The Communist Manifesto*?

Parrot fashion

?   *When Jack died, his African Grey parrot survived him and continues to deliver snatches of 'Tarrah, love' and 'By gum, in't it ready yet?' and other phrases of Jack's in a Yorkshire accent identical to Jack's. His wife finds this morbid and ghoulish. How shall I advise her ... the* Monty Python *route?*

What a shame to have stumbled on such a powerful business opportunity too late to make commercial use of it. If only a smart entrepreneur had had the foresight to persuade Peter Ustinov, Noel Coward or David Niven to play host to a few parrots. Then, once the birds had soaked up their master's voice, they could have been sold to people eager for a house companion capable of recounting anecdotes about playing polo with maharajahs, or about singing in pre-war Berlin with Marlene Dietrich, or about goofing off on location while filming *The Guns of Navarone*. The birds could entertain their new owners' friends with impersonations and gossip and even a song or two ('Even Liberace we assume, does it. Let's do it, let's fall in love . . .').

But cohabiting with an African Grey that mimics your late husband's everyday chit-chat, and in his accent? Not only is it not quite the same thing, it might distress any grieving widow. The *Monty Python* route seems severe. Donating him to a new home would certainly move the parrot out of the widow's earshot. But she might feel it to be a kind of avian adultery to think of her late husband as, albeit only via his undeceased parrot, making marital small talk to another woman.

Perhaps a friend – you? – might take in the African Grey as a lodger until it has learnt some new dialogue before returning it, reprogrammed, to the widow. You could even train it on old recordings of Ustinov on *Parkinson*.

A little German history

A friend recently married a German woman, who is now applying for a British passport. She asked me to sign her passport documents to verify that she is the woman pictured in the submitted photo. But I have known her for only one year, not the mandatory two years required by the authorities. I have no doubts about her authenticity, but am reluctant to break the law.

If all you are being asked to do is verify that your friend's wife is the woman pictured in the photograph accompanying her passport application (rather than, say, vouch for her character), then you'd have thought that knowing her for even a few months would be enough to give you the necessary authority to sign her papers; assuming, of course, that your eyesight is in good shape. Signing might be breaking the letter of the law, but hardly the spirit of it.

So why do you suppose that the authorities ask for two years' acquaintance with a passport applicant? Maybe now that cosmetic procedures carried out even during a lunch hour can produce quite startling shifts in appearance, they feel that a person's face can change dramatically in a single year (Joan Rivers' face can change almost hourly). Thus having to find a witness who has known you for at least two years heightens the chances of the witness being sure that the passport-seeker in the photograph really is the person whose name is on the application form.

Or maybe the staff in the passport office are just mischievous and they're paying back your friend's German wife for the years they spent at school in German lessons waiting for the verb finally to arrive at the end of a sentence (which, if it didn't take two years, often felt like it).

Fawn chorus

? *A friend who is a popular after-dinner speaker makes obsequious and flattering remarks, which I know he does not mean, about members of the audience. This leaves those mentioned with a warm glow, and also well-disposed towards him. Such fawning, false, unctuous behaviour irritates me. Should it? The speaker is bringing happiness to others as well as to himself.*

What an absolutely marvellous query! I can't tell you how rare it is to find a point made so eloquently, yet also so succinctly. You have put your finger on a key aspect of modern life. I'll bet that you're a jolly handsome fellow too, eh?

Mild flattery helps to lubricate the world: it's an excess of flattery, shovelled like manure on to a vegetable patch, that has us all skidding around unattractively in horse poop. Even you may occasionally have remarked admiringly on a frock that makes its wearer look as if she's dressed in a collage made by a six-year-old in art class; or told someone how cute their new baby daughter is, even though the person she most reminds you of is Leonid Brezhnev.

We all sometimes say to people's faces what we wouldn't say about them behind their backs: diplomats even get paid to do it. Actors and authors are keen for criticism, so long as it comprises unalloyed praise: the purpose of such flattery is to say to these actors and writers what their last iota of modesty prevents them from saying publicly about themselves.

Your friend is shameless, but mostly harmless. His targets may be wise to his game yet still happy to soak up his flattery, much the way a rich old goat might bury any qualms he has about why he is being fawned over by a woman as pneumatic as Anna Nicole Smith.

Lacking confidence

A friend whose companion, a driver, could suffer loss of consciousness at any time, revealed this information, in confidence, to my wife. Should my wife break that confidence? If so, to whom?

I know this might sound bone-headed on first reading, but the person to whom your wife should break that confidence is the friend who entrusted her with it in the first place.

Certainly, it is unethical to betray a confidence; even if you were to break it after having decided that to stay silent would be morally worse (if you heard of an assassination plan, say). But your wife can keep a clear conscience, and also do what's best, simply by persuading this friend that they must confront their partner. Otherwise that partner might end up on a hospital slab with a name tag around their big toe. Of course, it might not turn out like this. It might be that the friend and partner both end up in a mortuary, if the friend happened to be a passenger when their partner blacked out at the wheel.

It's possible that the friend, in sharing this confidence, was hoping your wife would urge them to tackle their partner; even offering tips on how to broach the issue sensitively, but firmly. It's like when women emerge from a shop's changing room and ask you: 'Does my bum look big in this?' They ask only if they have already decided that it does, and already know, in their hearts, that they will not be buying this dress. If a woman has really fallen in love with a frock, you could tell her that her bum looks as if she's hiding Orson Welles in the back of her knickers and she'd buy it just the same. Only when, later, she falls out of love with the dress might she reproach you for never having informed her how big her bum looks in it.

Going potty

? *A friend and I bought ten individual yoghurt pots to share equally. Today my friend took a pot from our communal fridge only to find that it had gone off. Now he expects us to share the last yoghurt as it was just his bad luck to choose a bad one. I believe that I have no moral obligation to give up my last yoghurt. How should we resolve this issue?*

I'm guessing with firearms. It sounds that serious.

It would be fairest to share the last yoghurt. Though this might not seem the optimum outcome for one of you (whoever it was who bagged the final extra yoghurt), it would be the least unpalatable solution for both of you.

But consider this: had you known in advance that one pot of the ten was rotten, you could have deduced which that pot was and thus stolen a march on your friend. The only requirement for this exercise is that you acknowledge that it will always be a surprise which pot turns out to be the one containing off yoghurt (which it obviously would, because the pots are opaque and sealed). Logically, then, it can't be the tenth and final pot that would be off, because by then it wouldn't be a surprise: if the first nine had been OK, you'd know it was the tenth that was off. But if it can't be the tenth that's rotten, nor can it be the ninth, because after eight OK pots you'd then be expecting that (having already ruled out the possibility of it being the tenth pot that had curdled), and it wouldn't be a surprise. Using similar logic, it can't be the eighth pot, nor the seventh, nor the sixth, nor the fifth, fourth, third, second, or first.

So though you know that one pot is off, and it will always be a surprise which pot that is, you can also logically deduce that none of the pots is off. Toying with this famous paradox will provide you and your friend with far more enjoyment than squabbling over yoghurt.

Surprising behaviour

We had an unexpected visit from a couple we had not seen for more than two years because they live far away. They were in the area, and had some time to spare. My husband ignored them, believing that as he had not invited them he was not obliged to entertain them. I told my husband that he had been rude. He says it was our guests who were rude.

It can make you feel slightly uncomfortable, when travelling abroad, to see how welcoming people can be to strangers. They invite them into their homes, feed them, offer them beds for the night, maybe skip work for the day to show off the sights of their home town, and in parts of Arkansas they may even let the visitors sleep with all their relatives. And livestock.

Many British folk have a knack of being able to soak up this hospitality with relish, while simultaneously incubating a tiny germ of panic deep in their soul.

This germ says: 'What if our hosts happen to be passing through the UK – maybe not this year or next, but they're bound to one day, aren't they? – and they phone us, obviously exploring the possibility of our reciprocating their hospitality? Will they believe me if I say that we're just off to a wedding: in Australia? What if I say we've all been struck down by flu and are in quarantine? Or should I – the minute I recognise their foreign accents – pretend to be the answering machine?'

Many other countries have a far more welcoming attitude to

unannounced visitors than we do. It is not uncommon for friends and relatives to drop by just because they happen to be passing. Might we not emulate this charming warmth? Yes, an unexpected visitor ringing your doorbell may derail your schedule; but mostly they brighten up what was going to be a predictable Sunday afternoon.

chip shot

While I was playing roulette at a casino, the croupier accidentally left one chip of mine behind after I had lost. My friend threw the chip on the table and by chance won on the next spin of the wheel. Should I have accepted the prize money? Should I have shared it with my friend?

Boy, your luck just goes on and on, doesn't it? First you are at a table with the only croupier in the world who leaves chips uncollected on the baize. Then you have a nimble-fingered friend who is brazen enough to steal the chip back slyly, and who is then lucky enough to toss that chip bang into the very middle of a numbered square (rather than, say, at the intersection of four numbers, which would have shrunk your winnings greatly).

And then? And then you are lucky enough for the ball to land on that very number when the dozy croupier next spins it around the roulette wheel. With that kind of good fortune shining down on you, you should be capitalising on your luck while it lasts: by volunteering to locate Osama bin Laden's hiding place, or by buying a Lottery ticket, or by phoning a computer technical helpline and finding (a) that you have got through to someone in less than forty-seven minutes and (b) that you have found the one assistant working for a technical helpline who can construct sentences in which at least two of the words exist in dictionaries.

It may feel as though there is a natural justice in pulling a fast one over a casino, because the odds are stacked heavily in its favour; and, after all, you're only raking back some of what you've lost, so the house is still up on balance. But it's still deceit. Some people are born lucky; some achieve luck; and some have luck thrust upon them. You just stole your luck.

Cat flap

> *I had planned to visit an old friend and his family for a few days on Boxing Day. I know he had gone to a great deal of trouble to provide for us. Alas, my cat was badly injured in a fight. Boarding her at a vet's while we were away would have cost £25 a night, so we cancelled the visit. My friend was very annoyed. Have I done wrong?*

A problem with cats is that, early in their lives, they take a huge tumble from a second-storey window and can't quite believe they're still alive when they hit the ground. They behave a little more cautiously for a while. But then they get hit by a scooter, and yet still manage to pad away unharmed. From then on they just assume that all those *Tom and Jerry* cartoons in which they've seen Tom regularly plummet off mountains, or get diced up in a Magimix, or ingest an ignited stick of dynamite, and survive, must be more reportage than far-fetched fiction.

From then on cats assume they really do have nine lives and can afford to live dangerously. They start staying out late and picking fights, just like Tom in *Tom and Jerry*, and *Top Cat*, and Liam Gallagher. But short of enrolling her in self-defence classes to improve her chances of coming out the victor in a scrape, you can't be blamed for your cat's behaviour.

But as regards your friend? Having accepted his invitation, and thus cost him money and effort, you had a moral duty to do your best to show up. A two-night stay for your cat at the vet's might have been the most upright solution, if you could have afforded it. Maybe you should factor in such expenses as part of the cost of owning a cat, much as you might factor in dry-cleaning bills as part of the cost of being one of Liam Gallagher's drinking buddies.

Found wanting

> *I am plagued by friends and relatives who know my interests but who, when buying me presents, never ask what I might actually want, or might already possess. I'd like a present and not a 'surprise'! Am I being ungrateful?*

The people to blame for your unrewarding haul of presents are not the gift-givers, but the gift-makers. It's like this: after a few years of buying presents for those to whom we are close, we've covered the known range of their likes. So rather than begin the same cycle of presents over again, we scour the shops for guidance. This is when gift-seekers notice paperweights.

Now, these shoppers know that they themselves have never needed a paperweight, working, as they do, in an office with the windows closed. But there are so many paperweights, in so many different shops, that they assume that perhaps their own writing regime is a little abnormal. Maybe, they start wondering, most other people write their letters at a desk planted on Whitstable beach in November. Thus they buy someone a gift of a paperweight because they mean well, but don't know better.

So be forgiving. I bet you've erred similarly yourself. Maybe you've bought someone a *Coldplay* CD because, seeing so many in the shops, you assumed that they must be popular – not realising that this music is used mostly by riot police to disperse crowds.

coarse companion

? *Our group of friends includes a woman who persistently puts others down, always deriding anything they say or do. Should we be rude back, or accept that she has an inferiority complex? She has some good qualities, and we do not wish to upset her very nice husband.*

Unless you're Gore Vidal, or Dorothy Parker, or Groucho Marx, or Mark Twain, chances are your insults and put-downs won't be amusing enough for people to forgive your rudeness.

Some people are born rude; the rest of us have rudeness thrust upon us. The trouble is that the people who cultivate rudeness often think they sound as amusing as Oscar Wilde, when they mostly just sound boorish. Take the historian David Starkey – *please!* When he speaks his inner voice must hear a laughter track like the one they superimpose on desperate TV sitcoms. To the rest of us, Starkey just sounds angry; as if he's in the TV studio under duress, and is saying what he has to say as briskly and as brusquely as possible so that he can take his leave all the more quickly to attend to some excruciatingly painful haemorrhoids.

Television bears some blame for this infection of rudeness.

Simon Cowell, for instance, has made a fat living from saying the sort of things to people's faces that would get him shot in parts of Los Angeles. Now even the successful tycoons on a TV show such as *Dragons' Den* feel they can't reject a budding entrepreneur's shaky business idea without also humiliating him or her.

We are all rude at times; only some of us regret it. Suggest that your friend channels her rudeness for profit. If joining the judging panel on *Pop Idol* is aiming too high, she could always settle for working in the customer relations department of almost any corporation.

Free Love

> **?** *We booked a holiday with friends, making a party of nine. The girlfriend of our friends' son has since decided to come along, utilising the 'free' place offered by the travel agency for every ten booked. But I was surprised when our friends told us that the cost of the holiday was unchanged – the total being still divided between nine, rather than ten. Is that fair?*

It's bad enough when you go on holiday with friends and return home a fortnight later unable to communicate except through your lawyers. But to be on the brink of frosty relations with your fellow-holidaymakers before the holiday has even begun . . . that can't bode well, can it?

I foresee a relaxing two weeks ahead – spent either apportioning restaurant bills down to the last grissino to the point where nearby diners wonder whether maybe you're conducting a tax audit, or else breezily agreeing to split restaurant bills ten ways, then privately seething when someone abuses this gesture by always ordering the lobster. (The next night someone else gets even by having fillet steak. Someone subsequently tops this by ordering caviar. By the end of the holiday your dining bills are so huge that the waiter needs to phone Mastercard for special authorisation.) Sharing the travel agent's invoice equally between all ten of you would be the most equitable way to split the holiday's cost, although your friends might argue that their son's girlfriend would not be able to afford to join the party were she expected to pay a one-tenth share, and so the cost to you would be the same whether she were to come or not.

But you might find non-monetary ways to enjoy the windfall; such as sharing the girlfriend.

Face-Saving reply

During a telephone conversation, an acquaintance and I talked briefly about the lovely products sold in a cosmetics shop near where she lives. Knowing that I do not have access to this shop, she sent me one of its products, worth £4.75. I was surprised to find the receipt attached. The item was unsolicited; do you think I should pay up?

On the downside, just by having idly mentioned in passing how much you liked a shop's range of cosmetics, you now find yourself the owner of £4.75 worth of cosmetics products you might have found appealing, but which you might not have bothered buying yourself. On the upside, you're lucky that you didn't idly mention to your acquaintance that you might like to own a house in her neighbourhood; or that you'd always wondered whether there was a strippergram company that provided male strippers the spitting image of Pavarotti.

It would have been nice if she'd gone the whole hog and sent you the item as a gift. But it's not as if she's seeking a profit from the transaction. The gesture was well-meant. If you want to make the exchange feel less commercial, then rather than post her a cheque for £4.75, send her something of similar value. That way, she'll feel her kind turn was repaid with another. Or else she'll learn how it feels to be sent something that was never requested.

At least she's only an acquaintance, that is, someone you know just about well enough for them not to be a stranger. With acquaintances, your irritation soon fades. With a friend, it would grate far more that someone so close could act so thoughtlessly. Paradoxically, we nurse grievances against friends far longer than we do against people we barely care about.

Small beer

A friend bought me a drink because an ATM cash machine had swallowed my card and I had no money. The next day I paid for his usual drink, which was cheaper. Should I have done only that, or should I have paid him the difference as well?

If you borrow £100 from a friend, you have a financial as well as a moral obligation to reimburse him or her the full £100. If your friend buys you a drink in a bar, you should buy him one in return; not necessarily that night, but you should be keeping an approximate tally of each other's hospitality – not so much because you are accountants, but because, as friends, neither of you would wish to slide into a state in which you were thought to be taking advantage of the other. The obligation is to return a favour rather than to fine-tune the finances to the nearest penny; otherwise it's not friendship but book-keeping.

But to order consistently only champagne when your friend drinks only halves of shandy is not a socialist slant on friendship ('From each according to his turn to buy the round; to each according to his palate'). It is, rather, a selfish slant on friendship. A quaffer of champagne doesn't knowingly and wilfully get a shandy-sipping friend to subsidise his pricier tastes.

Alcohol, as Benjamin Franklin wisely spotted, is proof that God loves us and wants us to be happy. We drink with friends because it cheers us; and because when you go for a medical and your urine sample is so toxic that the doctor plants a cocktail umbrella in it, you can assure him, truthfully, that you drink only socially. But you can continue to drink socially only if you avoid slipping into the habit of your favourite drink being whatever a friend treats you to.

Not to be sniffed at

Some friends, when they visit, bring us strong-smelling flowers, to which my wife and I are allergic. Do we accept gracefully, then throw the blooms away later? Or tell the friends as nicely as possible to take them home?

When your friends bring you flowers, they are showing that they think warmly enough of you to want to express it with a present, that they chose to show this affection by buying you something that will lift your spirits whenever you look at it, and that they were generous enough to spend money on getting you this something, rather than recycling a crocheted tissue-box holder they received from someone else, a practice now more common than cat fleas. Re-gifting is the modern version of those chain letters: you send a recycled gift to the person at the top of the list and, three months later, if everyone sticks to the rules, you're inundated with gifts that have been around the world more times than Henry Kissinger.

Buying you flowers is not a complex transaction. It's a token of friendship. Unless your allergy to the flowers is life-threatening, you should accept them not merely with grace, but with pleasure and enthusiasm. What end could possibly be served by your binning the flowers after your friends have left? Why not just pass them on to neighbours whose noses aren't as sensitive as your own?

Your friends will have been rewarded just by glimpsing some joy in your faces. They won't lose sleep if you then put the flowers in your shed until they wilt. On the other hand, being asked to take a gift home, however well-meant, is as churlish as accepting a generous invitation for dinner, but then asking your hosts whether you can bring your own food.

Prized friendship

I attend football games with two friends and usually buy a half-time draw ticket, agreeing to share any winnings. At a recent match we won £420. But we had taken another friend (because one of us was unable to go) and gave him a third of the amount. When our absent friend complained, we split it four ways. Was this fair?

You were wrong (well, thoughtless) to exclude a friend who had been such a long-standing partner in your informal syndicate. But your excluded friend was wrong to insist on his share even while absent; much as he might have liked to be included – not just for the obvious financial bonus, but also for the reassurance it would give him that he was an intimate member of your long-standing threesome, whether present in person or only in spirit.

You behaved correctly, and generously, by embracing your stand-in matchgoer in your syndicate. You again behaved correctly, and generously, by subsequently splitting your jackpot four ways to include your absent friend. Your actions don't make you a Henry Kissinger yet; but they do show that a little simple diplomacy, blended with a bit of give-and-take, can pay long-term rewards without necessarily demanding huge sacrifices (resort to dropping napalm on the natives only when all else has failed).

Of course, if you found your absent friend's demands for a slice of the pot a little grasping in the circumstances, you might still consider it diplomatically worthwhile to cut him in on the action until you can devise a sterner way to convey your displeasure and get even. As Will Rogers said: 'Diplomacy is the art of saying "Nice doggie" until you can find a rock.'

Meat the guests

? *At Sunday lunch with friends, the newly vegetarian wife produced a superb beef casserole for her husband and guests, but ate veggieburgers herself. Her husband was thrilled to have guests for lunch: it meant that he could eat meat again. When returning the invitation, should I prepare a vegetarian meal for us all, or cook meat, along with a separate vegetarian meal for the wife?*

There's nothing wrong with being a vegetarian. But as a vegetarian you must also accept that though you may like to see animals frolicking freely around a field, many others like to see theirs served medium-rare, with chips and green beans on the side. Nobody ever says: 'Hey, if you're really not eating your bean sprouts, would you mind if I nabbed them?' And, anyway, it's worth bearing in mind that most of the animals we eat – cows, lambs – are grass-eaters, so we're all vicarious vegetarians in a way.

On the other hand, vegetarians are shamefully treated. Waiters rarely know whether what is described as a vegetarian stew contains meat stock; many restaurants think that if they remove the bits of chicken from a bowl of noodles it can pass as vegetarian. Even shops sell meals that look as if they're meat-free until you spot at the very end of the ingredients list that they contain gelatine: why would you exclude half your market like that?

Most vegetarians are very accommodating; they don't expect hosts to make a special effort but are always grateful when they do. Your friend might be touched that you prepared a wholly vegetarian meal. Equally, she might feel uncomfortable that everyone else is having to eat nut rissoles purely on her account.

7 Just Lending A Hand

'We are here on earth to do good for others; what the others are here for I have no idea'

W.H. Auden

Reading the Situation

I am pained by the plight of the homeless on London's streets, but am unsure how best to help. Is it preferable to buy them food, as opposed to simply giving them money? How sensitive, or insensitive, is it to buy them a book? They must get bored sitting there all day.

If you're about to give a homeless person a few coins, some people will say to you, 'Why are you giving them money? They'll spend it on export-strength lager and cigarettes.' They often say things like this while they are themselves sucking a Marlboro, on their way to the pub.

If you have a decent job; if you wear clothes that fit you, while not simultaneously making you look as if you've dressed for a casting for members of Fagin's gang in a production of *Oliver*; and you don't smell as if you're experimenting with a novel way of smoking kippers by incubating a herring under each of your armpits, chances are that you have a less urgent need to block out the chilly world with nicotine and export-strength lager than have many homeless people. (Who was it, anyway, who decided that regular lager was good enough for the domestic population, but that drinkers overseas crave 'export-strength' ale with the sort of alcohol content that allows the beer to double as a local anaesthetic?)

Many believe it is better to donate to charities that care for the homeless than to give directly to the homeless themselves. Maybe. But when you're handing a few coins to someone living in a cardboard box, you're salving your own conscience as much as helping them out. Were you setting them up with a trust fund, it might seem reasonable to seek a say in how they spend it. To donate £1 and impose your taste in food or literature on them seems needlessly impertinent.

Dogged by doubt

For animal-welfare reasons, my husband and I try to eat humanely raised organic meat. Should we then buy organic meat for our dog? The vet recommends, for health reasons, a diet of white meat and fish, but my husband buys her cheap broiler chickens. Would it be unnatural, and unethical, to put her on a vegetarian diet?

Do you have any idea what a dog will happily put into its mouth? It's organic, all right. It's not just a question of it being Soil Association approved. Much of it is soil.

Dogs were raised by their parents in a canine-consumer culture of try-before-you-buy. They are willing to taste pretty much anything, before either spitting it out or swallowing it. Even after years of watching their dogs, many owners would be reluctant to put money on which items their dog will reject and which they will happily ingest.

Thinkers from Aristotle through Descartes to Kant all more or less thought animals were dumb beasts beyond the reach of ethical consideration; you need not share their outlook to realise that feeding a pet an organic fillet steak veers more towards indulgence than morality. Buy yourself organic meat if it makes you feel better. But putting your dog, too, on an organic diet is a long way from feeding her white meat and fish for health reasons. Concern for animals does not simply mean 'do unto dogs as you would have done unto yourself'. Otherwise, why stop at serving your pet organic poussin? Why not also napkins, and a fine Beaune?

Much as you love your pet, you have to remember that it's not actually human. That's why it's called a dog. As for resolving your organic-meat dilemma by putting the animal on a soul-sapping vegetarian diet, that's like resolving a dilemma over whether to allow your dog to have sex once a month or thrice a week by having her spayed. In fact, spaying is vegetarian for sex.

Shop soiled

I give money to a shabbily-dressed homeless woman who sits outside my local, upmarket grocery. One day she asked if I would add her grocery items to my basket because the store would not let her shop there. Two managers were glaring at me from behind her. What should I do?

Test their resolve to see who blinks first. If the shop refuses to allow you to buy her groceries alongside your own, it's because they reckon they probably won't be too much out of pocket: they reckon that they can afford to make a stand. If, on the other hand, you were to send the homeless woman into the store, having first asked her to add your full shopping list to her own modest grocery requirements, the shop's sharp-suited managers might think twice about losing all your custom if they refused her entry.

You wonder what makes store managers so picky, given some of the people they do let into their premises. If you're going to vet customers for dress, how about also checking their maths to see whether they can count to ten before letting them join the 'ten items or fewer' express checkout? If they truly cared about customers, shop managers would also place all those items that 98 per cent of shoppers come to buy within a metre of the entrance, instead of hiding them among seventeen aisles, as if grocery shopping were a kind of elaborate treasure hunt.

Adding the woman's few items to your own shopping is unlikely to threaten your welcome at the store, however grumpy the managers. The only way it could be risky to do her shopping would be if she asked you to buy her some sirloin from the top shelf of the meat counter – the only legitimate circumstances in which you could tell her: 'No, the steaks are too high.'

Losing your bottle

We continue to have milk delivered (even though the bottle tops tend to leak when laid flat) because my wife, a GP, is worried that doorstep milk delivery might stop if demand falls, making it hard for the elderly to get fresh milk; and because I want to buy milk in recyclable containers. Are these ethically valid reasons to spurn the more convenient supermarket cartons?

Man's failure to devise an attractive, trouble-free container for milk seems sometimes like the cow's revenge against mankind for daring to interfere with its intimate body parts. Lord knows, cows made it tricky enough for man to even locate their milk; hiding it down there, and in such a scary-looking pouch. You wonder who ever thought of pinching a cow's teats and then volunteering to drink the liquid that squirted from them, the same way you wonder who first looked at an artichoke and thought, 'Well, *this* certainly looks edible!' Glass bottles from a doorstep-delivery milkman that leak when laid on their side, those cartons with wings that snap open like Cubist origami, the newer cartons with grenade-style ring-pulls, plastic supermarket flasks – the only milk container worse than these is those miniature peel-back-the-foil-and-pour milk tubs they hand you on planes which barely contain enough milk for your coffee even before you've spilt half of the tub's contents over your lap.

But your wife is right: we must make a stand for what we value. Country-dwellers whine when their village shop closes, having never provided it with the sort of custom that might have kept it afloat. Your wife's concern for the welfare of her elderly neighbours is a worthy motive to stick with your milkman. You could always stand the bottles upright. Or buy a pet cow.

Dolly mixture

? *I want to buy our child's toys from charity shops because we get through them so quickly. My wife says that we should leave them for those who are in greater need of cheap toys. I say that if nobody buys them, the charity does not raise any money at all, which is surely the purpose of charity shops selling goods. Who is right?*

You really want to save money on your child's toys? Buy them a London Underground train set. This way you won't have to buy any trains at all. You simply poke your head around the child's bedroom door every so often to announce why the trains are delayed (signal failure, a centimetre of snow, too much sunshine . . . almost anything goes) and why they may never arrive before it's time for bed/school/ballet. What could be cheaper? And such an easily transportable toy! While waiting for the phantom trains, get the child to scribble down numbers to compile a train timetable. No matter if they produce a jumble of figures that bears no relation to any real-life train movements. That just makes the timetable look all the more authentic!

As for charity shops, you and your wife are not in conflict. You want to keep toy expenditure to a minimum because your child outgrows toys so quickly, while also ensuring that charity shops earn revenue they can divert to good works. Your wife wants less well-off parents to be able to visit charity shops stocked with toys they can afford. Both aims are laudable. They are not mutually exclusive.

If you bought toys from charity shops, you would be providing them with income. If you donated these toys back to charity shops after your child had outgrown them, they would still be available for less well-off parents to buy, while providing a repeat tide of revenue for the charity shops.

Going for a song

When I was visited by carol singers, two tuneless teenage girls, I asked what they were collecting for. They answered: 'Ourselves.' I pointed out that carol singing is a way of collecting for charity, which surprised them, and I gave nothing. Was I being uncharitable?

What a marvellous Christmas story! You educated these girls about the true purpose of carol-singing: a way of raising money for charity while bringing cheer to the doorsteps of neighbours who might be housebound, and thus unable to visit a local supermarket to hear carols being pumped at bullhorn volume from the loudspeaker system. Meanwhile, these girls also learnt an important lesson that they'll nurse for the rest of their lives – that it's easier to get what you want if you just brazenly lie.

Chances are that if the girls had lied and told you that they were singing carols to raise money for the homeless, you would have handed them a few coins. So by being honest with you, they have been exposed as behaving immorally. But had they behaved immorally and lied to you, they'd have got what they wanted and you would have thought them saintly.

Who knows what people do with the money for which they ask us with the noblest of intentions? We often wonder this, too, about our council tax collectors.

Having learnt their lesson, these girls probably then told your neighbours that they were singing for charity and were handsomely rewarded. It's the same cheeky trick politicians use on gullible voters at the doorstep to get themselves elected. Far from being uncharitable, you may have set these girls on the path to political office.

Exercising discretion

At my gym I noticed an overweight man attempting (inexpertly) an advanced form of sit-up that should be tried only by the experienced. As a physiotherapist, I knew that, at best, the exercise would not benefit him; at worst, it could damage his back or give him a hernia. But I felt loath to interfere at the risk of causing insult or embarrassment. Should I have?

Some people are lucky. They manage to keep trim without needing to exercise. A Russian dissident can shed half a stone in sweat just by hearing that he's been invited to President Putin's Valentine's Day sushi party. The rest of us have to work harder at it; at any rate, those of you who don't follow my own failsafe body-enhancement regimen of never standing naked in front of a full-length mirror.

Do gyms even make any sense? You spend twenty minutes cruising for a parking place as near as you can get to the gym's entrance so that you can spend the next hour on a Stairmaster. We invent remote controls to save us walking a few feet to the TV set, then go jogging for several miles.

It's not as if you even lose any actual weight. It just gets transferred to different places. Take male gym-goers. All their weight migrates to their necks. That's what all that pumping is for. They can't wear polo-neck sweaters because they don't know any more where their head ends and their neck starts. If you are a qualified physiotherapist and you spot a man potentially doing himself an injury, you should feel no embarrassment in discreetly alerting him to it. It's much more grown-up than pointing and sniggering.

Dog-eat-dog world

An animal-loving friend who has two cats and a dog, and who also feeds the cat of a neighbour who is in hospital, puts out feed for two mice living in her garden wall so that they do not have to go far to eat, and might thus avoid being caught by the cats. I think she is merely fattening the mice for an eventual kill by the cats. Was I wrong not to talk her out of this?

It is always tricky to know whether to halt the workings of Mother Nature. On the one hand, we might save a life – say, of a gazelle that is being chased by a lion, even if we are only delaying that gazelle's death or possibly just forcing the lion to target a different gazelle. On the other hand, had we not let Nature run its course unhindered, the world would have been denied the entertainment of the Bill Clinton and Monica Lewinsky saga.

By cossetting the mice, your friend may instead just be signing the death warrant of a visiting bird, or of a less pampered mouse venturing from another neighbour's garden in search of supper. If she is aiming to protect the mice so that they might eventually die of old age, then your friend means well, even if she is unlikely to be successful. But why has she chosen to take the side of a mouse over that of a cat, which also has a stomach that needs filling?

And how does she know that she is not turning these mice into the equivalent of slovenly couch potatoes who have grown accustomed to regular pizza deliveries while they loll about all day doing nothing? How does she know that mice don't enjoy the thrill of the chase, however risky, the same way that climbers enjoy trying to conquer Everest, even though they know they are risking their lives in the attempt? Who's to say that her wall-guests wouldn't rather live one day as a tiger than a year as a mouse? Even if they are mice!

Pipe tobacco

Despite her diabetes, our daily help (now a family friend) smokes twenty cigarettes a day. When I go abroad she insists that I bring her back duty-free cigarettes and she pays me at cost. I hate doing this and I press her to give up smoking. She threatens to resign if I don't do so. Our friends say that she has the right to kill herself and that supplying the cigarettes makes no difference. What do you say?

Cigarettes are legal. You are not procuring proscribed narcotics. At worst, you might be subsidising a premature death that she has already chosen for herself. But you are her employer (and her friend), not her keeper. Would you feel similarly torn if she pestered you for an artery-clogging Sachertorte the next time you visited Vienna? Or feel protective of her mental wellbeing if she were to ask you, the next time you are in New York, to bring her back a photograph of David Gest?

You could rid yourself of your dilemma by finding a new cleaner. If it's fear of finding a good replacement that's stopping you, then you have no moral leg to stand on. If you don't want her to go because she is now a friend, then as a friend you should offer advice but not feel responsible if she refuses to heed it.

All human beings have faults: friends are people whose faults we know, yet like nonetheless. Everyone appreciates a second opinion (unless it is: 'Tom's right. Your date *IS* ugly!'). Nobody likes a nag.

Since your friend will smoke no less even without your connivance, and since her earnings are unlikely to be in the Rockefeller class, then saving her a few pounds on tobacco allows her a few otherwise unaffordable treats. Far from being evidence of moral dereliction, your cigarette runs might be seen as a moral duty.

Trashy behaviour

I use the recycling facilities at a large supermarket for items that are not collected from my home. But the supermarket is in another county. My own county provides similar facilities, but at its waste depot, which would require me to make a special journey. Is it unethical to recycle through another county when I don't pay it any council tax?

If you believe in the virtues of recycling, you must presumably believe that being ecologically-minded means being blind to such man-made frontiers as county borders. This may explain why items that we send for recycling in London can end up being shipped halfway around the world to landfills in the Far East: in an age when we are urged to trim our use of air travel to reduce our carbon footprint, old wine bottles and empty Weetabix cartons are now becoming better-travelled than humans.

It might offend a county's accountant to see his county footing the recycling bill for goods dumped by people from whom the county receives no tax revenue, but it surely defeats the purpose to drive an air-polluting ten miles to a waste depot for the sake of fiscal neatness.

As the economist John Maynard Keynes said, give a man a

lump of coal and he'll keep himself warm for an evening – give him a nuclear power plant with Homer Simpson at the controls and he could wipe out a whole continent. (No, wait. I'm not sure that Keynes did actually say that.) Anyway, the point is that we're all in this together, recycling where we can, allowing for some give-and-take. It is hardly in your neighbouring county's interest to police its recycling facilities if the upshot is that it shares air currents with a county so polluted that it smells like a chip-pan fire.

Huffing and puffing

While drinking coffee at a local establishment I noticed a lady at a far table smoking. Just as I was about to protest – the café being non-smoking – I noticed that she was in a wheelchair. I decided that, as her pleasures were limited, I'd do nothing. Was I right or wrong?

I'd say you were wrong. The last thing a person in a wheelchair needs (ranking just after being talked to in a VERY LOUD VOICE, on the assumption that people in wheelchairs also suffer impaired hearing) is being patronised by a stranger who knows nothing about them. If you were going to pity people, where would it end? With Mel Gibson? George Galloway?

We all, whether walking or wheelchair-bound, would wish to be treated equally by others: that includes being ticked off if we offend. Otherwise robberies would be a doddle: bank-robbers wouldn't need guns, just an accomplice in a wheelchair as insurance against prosecution. (Judge: 'OK, the defendant did steal £4 million from the bank. But then again, she is in a wheelchair – so let's just call it high jinks, eh?') As for your deciding that this smoker's other pleasures were limited, you should know that there are many people in wheelchairs who lead far fuller lives than people who have legs like a wallaby's. The frontier between being thoughtfully considerate, on the one hand, and pitying or patronising somebody, on the other, may be slender, but it is also heavily land-mined.

If you wouldn't patronise someone for being a woman, or a Catholic, or a Jew, or for being black, or white, or a lawyer, then why patronise them just for being in a wheelchair? If the woman was smoking, and shouldn't have been, why not just ask her politely to stub it out?

Going flat out

While driving down a narrow country lane at its 20mph limit, I let a tailgating car overtake me and race past. After a few bends, we came upon a newly squashed rabbit. If it had been squashed by that speeding driver, was I responsible? Since I believe that animals should be killed only if you are going to eat them, did I have a moral duty to take the rabbit home and cook it?

We city folk are often shocked when driving in the countryside to see how the natives throw their cars around. The narrower the road, the faster country-dwellers seem to drive. It's as if they are responding to some law of physics whereby the same volume of car squeezed into a narrower tube of road results in the car gaining speed of its own volition – like sticking your thumb over a garden hose and seeing the trickle of water turn into a dart as it races out of the suddenly constricted hose opening, as if it's on a mercy dash to douse the hydrangeas.

Had you not been on that road, the other driver would have been speeding anyway, and the rabbit would probably have been as dead as it was after you let the car overtake you. Though you were a player in the drama, you were hardly Hamlet. You were too far removed from the rabbit's death to bear responsibility.

It's a pretty senseless way to go, but then country animals must be used to it by now. They're always being run over, or eaten by something bigger or fiercer. That's why animals don't have funerals, or else you wouldn't be able to move in the countryside for slow-moving miniature hearses blocking up the lanes every day.

Whatever your beliefs, you do not have to eat every animal that is killed accidentally, or else you'd be licking windscreens clean at the end of every motorway. Leave the rabbit for a dog in the night-time.

Bag Lady

While I was lunching with a friend at a restaurant, a lady at an adjacent table asked: 'Would you mind looking after my bags while I go to the ladies?' We nodded that we would do so. A long time passed. My friend and I had finished our lunch and wished to leave. By nodding my assent, had I entered into some sort of contract, morally obliging me to watch the bags until her return?

When a woman says she is 'going to the ladies' she's using a code that even the men who cracked Enigma were never able to decipher. When scientists try to work out what might happen to time inside a black hole, they actually experiment with ladies' lavatories. A man can visit a public loo and be out again in minutes. A woman in a restaurant or bar can say she's 'going to the ladies' and by the time she reappears the country may have elected a new prime minister.

Still, you should have thought of all this before going along with her plan. It may sound like an innocuous enough request, 'Will you keep an eye on my bags while I go to the ladies?', but once you have agreed to it, you are committed. It's like a diluted version of an arranged marriage: you have made a commitment to stick with that stranger's bag through thick and thin, in sickness and in health, until such time as its owner shall return. (And not a Mickey Rooney or Elizabeth Taylor type of marriage vow, either; you know, the sort whereby you commit to keep an eye on this particular bag, but only until such time as a more enticing bag comes along.) Otherwise, what is the nature of your commitment to this stranger? That you will honour your pledge to guard her bag as long as it's convenient for you to do so? Surely that's as morally suspect as playing poker and agreeing to pay your debts so long as you're winning.

Organ stop

I have signed up to the organ donor register so that my body parts can be used after my death, and informed family and close friends of this decision. But can I request that my liver goes to someone who has not abused alcohol (I have not drunk alcohol for many years as I do not like the taste)? Or am I not entitled to any say in the matter of who receives which organ?

You embark on a precarious path when you do something as generous as offering your organs for donation so that others might live, but then start making judgements as to what kind of person might be worthy of these organs. It is easy enough to see why you might believe that someone who has soused their own liver in liquor might have less right to a second stab at life than someone who just happened, by a quirk of nature, to have been born with a faulty liver.

But where would you draw the line? Your heart can go to an athlete, but not to someone who put their own heart under strain by eating like a hog or by pursuing a stressful job? What about religions? Should an organ donor be able to dictate that they don't want their kidneys to end up in a Catholic/Jew/Muslim? Can a member of a neo-fascist political party insist that their lungs should only ever again fill with air inhaled by a fellow party member, who can live another day to spread the party's word? Should a pacifist be allowed to request that his heart not end up beating in the body of a soldier? What if a politician should need a new liver, would it be justifiable to deny him? What if it was an actor whose films you detested?

As it happens, the NHS-run Organ Donor Register confirms that you can choose which organs you donate, but cannot stipulate into whom these organs may, or may not, be transplanted.

Taking no one for a ride

I am an unpaid trustee of a national charity. This year's accounts showed an entry of £58 for 'one trustee's expenses for attending board meetings and the annual conference' – the very sum I claimed last year. Although the charity reimburses trustees' travel costs, it seems that no one else claims. Am I a lesser person for claiming when they do not?

If everybody's expenses claims were available for public scrutiny, you'd have very little to feel embarrassed about. You have only to stroll into any of the hundreds of crowded

242

restaurants at lunchtime in any major city in the world to realise that, when it comes to business expenses, there is a lot of creative accounting going on. If all these business lunches were leading to hot deals, then the world's GDP would be at least 247 times what it is today. Just knowing whether Donald Trump meets his hairspray bill out of his own pocket or whether he claims it on expenses could have a material bearing on his company's market value.

It's the fact of the amount of your expenses being a ho-hum £58 that muddies the issue. What if your expenses totalled £1.50? Ethics aside, you might think it not worth the bother of completing the paperwork to file such a small claim. But what if the total were £450? This sum is substantial enough not to be a trifle, and you might understandably infer that your worth as a trustee must be considerable or the charity would not be offering to reimburse you. Yet a claim of £450 would obviously be a far greater drain on the charity's resources than your current one for £58, let alone one for £1.50. But if it is ethically justifiable to claim £450, you should feel no guilt in asking for your £58 of travelling costs to be reimbursed.

Eye doctor

? *I'm a doctor with a good eye for skin cancer. When I see it in my patients, I tell them. I've diagnosed relatives' and neighbours' tumours. Sometimes I notice a tumour on the back of a stranger's head on a bus, but say nothing; I could be wrong and they could be traumatised. Is a doctor ever off duty?*

You may have stumbled on the last unexploited idea for a TV game show: *Spot the Disease*, in which medical specialists scour the streets for people afflicted with ailments of which they are unaware ('Yes, you, sir – you have kidney stones!'). Or maybe top physicians are teamed up with celebrities, as in *Strictly Dance Fever*, and are given eight weeks in which to tutor the celebrities in how to recognise life-threatening ailments?

Telling a woman that she has dropped her glove is one thing. Being told by a stranger that you have cancer? That's more intrusive. So should you repress your urge to speak your mind, as you might if you spotted an actor whose movies you thought stank (naming names is invidious; but let's say an actor with the initials 'SS', whose first name rhymed with Sylvester and his last with Stallone)?

Much as you might relish the thrill of detection and saving lives, you must also respect people's right to live in ignorance if they choose. Sugaring the pill by telling them that their tumour might be nothing is like telling Graham Norton that he comes across as a little camp – but, hey, that's just your opinion, and you could be wrong. If you saw a couple bickering in a shop, would you proffer marriage-counselling tips? Probably not. So some people might believe that you have no moral right to diagnose a stranger's skin cancer. You might equally argue that you have no moral right not to do so.

Skipping Lessons

? *There are usually one or two skips in my area and I am not above dumping things in them, usually at night. I justify this on the basis that when I hire a skip I do not object to other people doing the same thing. Indeed, I look on it as a form of collective community act. Am I justified in this?*

Behaving ethically is not simply a question of freely, and unguiltily, doing to others what you would happily allow them to do to you. You might as well say that you can see nothing intrinsically wrong in approaching Claudia Schiffer in broad daylight and licking her from head to toe, on the ground that you would not raise any objection were she to decide to do the very same thing to you. True, you should treat others as you would wish them to treat you. But that usually means: don't punch Mike Tyson if you wouldn't want him to punch you.

In the instance you describe, the relevant yardstick is not your degree of tolerance, or your broadmindedness, or your generosity, but the degree of tolerance of others. Reciprocity is certainly part of the equation. Give-and-take is a fine enough principle, if both parties agree. If one party is reluctant, then it just becomes take. Or, worse, an arrestable offence. You may not give yourself permission to camp with your family for the night in the gardens of Buckingham Palace just because you would happily let the Queen and the Duke of Edinburgh pitch their tent in your backyard if they happened to be in your neighbourhood.

If you feel so confident that you stand on firm moral ground, why not attach a note with your dumped sofas and bookshelves, detailing your name and address, and see whether the builders who hired the skip send you a thank-you note?

Pushing the envelope

? *At Christmas I hand an envelope to my postman, to my newspaper lady and to the bin team, each containing the same amount. But since my bins are collected by a team of at least three people, the money is not enough even for a round of drinks! Is this equitable, or am I being mean?*

You evidently look after your visitors well. Well enough, at any rate, not to find your post dumped in a roadside grit storage box; or your usual newspaper substituted 'in error' by a copy of the *Daily Sport*, featuring articles about women who have fallen in love with a chimp at the local zoo after watching Peter Jackson's *King Kong*, and who now subsist on a diet of banana milkshakes; nor to find your garden strewn with your neighbour's rubbish.

Yes, it does seem cruel that the binmen should have to share the same pot as the solo postman and newspaper lady. You always feel similarly sorry for musicians in those Glenn Miller-style big bands, who must divvy up between them the same cut of the box-office takings as solo artistes get to pocket all for themselves. See how much richer Sting and Robbie Williams became once they stopped having to share their royalties with fellow band members? Similarly, the success, longevity and solvency of the British monarchy may be due to the sovereign's astute decision to work as a solo artiste, thereby enabling the reigning monarch to keep all the spoils.

It is the responsibility of the binmen's employer to see that they are each remunerated sufficiently and equitably. Your duty is to pay the going rate for a tip, just as you would pay the same for a concert ticket whether it was for Tony Bennett or the New York Philharmonic.

Orchestra pits

A close friend plays in a barely adequate amateur orchestra. It performs often, to large (and not very

discerning) audiences, giving all proceeds to charity. My husband and I are quite musical and find the standard painful. Is it more ethical to lie that we have a fictitious prior commitment, or to attend and then lie when asked if we enjoyed the concert?

If we all attended only those musical concerts where the standard of playing and singing matched that of Covent Garden or La Scala, then kindergarten Christmas shows and most school concerts would have an audience consisting only of neatly-spaced rows of empty chairs.

Your moral duty to a friend overrides most other obligations, including the obligation to spare your ears the sort of aural assault that would make an angle-grinder sound like Mozart. If aesthetic judgements trumped our commitment and devotion to the wellbeing of our friends then, at art gallery openings, who would turn up to sip the warm *pinot grigio* from grimy wineglasses that had not been properly washed since their last party at the local sale-or-return liquor store? Dinner party tables would have empty seats where friends decided at the last minute that – much as they love their hosts – they couldn't be bothered spending an evening making conversation with people they had hitherto survived quite happily not knowing, and whom they will most probably never meet again. And nobody would be happily sponsoring people for large sums to do silly things for charities they had never heard of.

It is more moral to attend and lie. If you feel the need every now and then to give your ears some respite, then maybe show your commitment by donating a small sum anyway.

Running doubts

? *I recently sponsored an acquaintance for £30 to run in the London Marathon, all donations having been promised to his chosen charity. On the eve of the event he e-mailed to say that he would no longer be running because of injury. Since I have no way of verifying if the money will end up with a charity or in his pocket, would it be wrong of me to ask for it back?*

Marathon runners are famously prone to various afflictions: panting, gibbering, chafing inner thighs, nipples made sore by excessive friction. No, wait. I'm sorry. That's not marathon runners I was thinking of, it's John Prescott.

Presumably you are sponsoring this acquaintance not because you especially wish to see him suffer by running twenty-six miles, but because you wish to donate money to charity: his exertions are merely part of a cosy formula for cajoling cash from people for a worthy cause. If it was merely a question of paying someone to cover twenty-six miles, your friend could have done this in a taxi, thereby sparing himself weeks of training and Pavarotti-grade pasta consumption, and also the humiliation of scampering across London dressed in those skimpy shorts that look as if they've been made from a couple of tissues.

I recently sponsored a schoolboy doing a 'mathathon'. He and his classmates spent ten hours solving equations to raise money for charity. They could have done it with a calculator in twenty-five minutes, but that would hardly have been the point, would it?

We all know that marathon runners are dishonest. Who could honestly say that they run twenty-six miles and enjoy it? But having trusted him to hand your cash to a charity if he did run, there is no reason to doubt that your friend will do so, even though he was injured. Pay up.

chippy biker

> **?** *As I was travelling home on my motorcycle last week, at a set of traffic lights I heard one car driver ask another if there was a McDonald's nearby. The reply was 'Don't know'. I knew there was one just around the corner but, as I am strongly against junk food, did not provide the information. Should I have?*

You know, it's not actually illegal to eat in a McDonald's restaurant; much as you yourself might think twice about eating in any fast-food joint where you happen to believe that the food tastes the way Edward G. Robinson's face looks.

And it is always risky to jump to conclusions, if what you're jumping over is the facts. What if the inquirer were looking for a local branch of McDonald's not to fill his stomach with a giant burger and a serving of cola big enough to douse a brush fire, but because he wanted to discuss with the manager the possibility of his including a tofu option on the menu; or because he was planning to hand out samples of hoummos on hand-knitted whole-wheat to potential McDonald's customers, to encourage them to reconsider their diet and order the most wholesome menu options available; or even because the inquirer was about to ask the restaurant to serve (even) tastier food? If any of these was, indeed, the case, then your silence at the traffic lights would have produced precisely the opposite result to that which you intended.

Much as we might believe we know best, others are entitled to do as they wish, assuming that they are not breaking any law.

Imagine if you needed to know if there were a motorcycle repair shop nearby where you could fix your bike, and someone kept silent just because they regarded motorcycling as a stupidly dangerous activity?

Dead against it

? *For the funeral of a dear friend, the family requested that donations be made to two organisations – to both of which I am opposed. Cheques are being sent via the home, so if I 'forget' to send, or choose an alternative charity, this will be noticed and might upset the family. Am I behaving morally or selfishly?*

Funnily enough, last Christmas I decided to ask people what they wanted as presents, so as to avoid my handing them gifts which they would open on Christmas morning with a festive cry of, 'I can't believe that anyone would actually pay money for this!' And do you know what? Their taste turned out to be a big letdown.

A nephew asked for a James Blunt album. Oh my! So I gave him a *Bob Dylan's Greatest Hits* CD instead. A niece who requested an Avril Lavigne CD got a great Ella Fitzgerald collection of Cole Porter songs. My mother wanted a blue cardigan, but I thought that brown would suit her better. A vegetarian friend who said she had too many possessions asked me for an edible gift, so long as it wasn't meat! I told her she didn't realise what she was missing and sent her a whole prosciutto.

Hey, did I do wrong?

The cheque for charity is for your friend, not for you. How ugly could the chosen causes be for you to feel queasy at contributing? A neo-Nazi group? A racist organisation? If the deceased sympathised with such causes, how did he or she become such a dear friend in the first place? Flowers, or a charitable donation, are a way of marking your love and respect for the dead person. That includes respecting their wishes. Faced with a choice between abandoning a friend or your principles, you should ideally have the moral courage not to abandon a friend.

Nanny State

? *My neighbours' nanny plays happily in the garden with their three children, aged two to five, and takes them out most days. I'm sure that she does an excellent job. But when she bundles them into her car, she doesn't strap them in. Should I say something to my neighbours? My wife says it is none of my business.*

It is obvious why anyone might feel reluctant to interfere in their neighbours' affairs. Nobody likes a curtain-twitching busybody. But there is a difference between snitching and showing concern. For instance, whispering in Sylvester Stallone's ear that his mother, Jackie, looks as if her face is melting is snitching; whereas telling Jackie Stallone to her face that she'd be doing the world a favour if she could persuade her son to stop making more movies is showing concern.

Informing your neighbours that their childminder bundles their three young children into the back seat of her car without strapping them in with seatbelts might put your neighbours in an awkward position with regard to their nanny. But they would doubtless rather that than be in the awkward position of having to scrape their children off the inside of a car's windscreen.

It is hard to imagine that they would chastise you for interfering in their affairs, particularly if you mention that the nanny seems to be doing a good job in most other respects. Would you not wish to be alerted to such a risk to your children if you were in your neighbours' shoes? There are occasions when we all have to judge when a matter that is none of our business is nonetheless somehow our concern, however reluctant we are generally to interfere. Your wife is correct in principle, but in this case surely wrong in practice.

Park keeper

I frequently see people who are not disabled, and without disabled badges for their cars, parking in disabled spaces at my local supermarket. Is it justified for me to challenge them publicly? I did so recently and was met by total indifference on the part of the perpetrator.

Driving in general, and parking in particular, is the Las Vegas of the motoring world. Ever heard the American saying: 'What happens in Vegas, stays in Vegas'? It's a way of acknowledging that people's characters undergo inexplicable changes when they are surrounded by Las Vegas's twenty-four-hour neon, by casinos built like Ancient Rome, and by bald men from Topeka nuzzling so deeply in a hooker's cleavage that it looks to passers-by like the woman maybe possesses three breasts.

Once installed in Las Vegas, even the most timid men lose their inhibitions and self-restraint – they gamble away the family house; they sell a kidney for roulette chips; and worse, sometimes they stoop so low that they actually marry Britney Spears for a weekend, or even attend a Celine Dion concert.

When taunted by the challenge of finding an empty space

in a busy supermarket car park, many people succumb to Vegas syndrome: men and women who wouldn't normally even drop litter, or tread on an ant, feel no shame in steering their car into a slot reserved for the disabled. But that doesn't make it your moral responsibility 'to challenge them publicly'. Are you looking to save parking spaces for disabled shoppers, or to pick a fight? You are not a car park vigilante. You may be justified in pointing out their shamelessness, but not much more. Inform a member of the supermarket's staff. Maybe suggest that they introduce Vegas-style valet parking.

Cigarette tips

> *When I stopped smoking twenty-one months ago, I vowed to keep my stock of duty-free tobacco for two years: if I'd kicked the habit by then, I would either destroy the tobacco, or sell it at cost. With the two years now almost up, should I sell to a smoker, destroy it, or give it away to known smokers, saving them some money?*

The only trouble with giving up smoking is that you become something potentially worse: an ex-smoker. You no longer inflict passive smoking on those around you; just passive smugness. Bill Clinton managed to be a smug ex-smoker without even having smoked, famously stating that while he might have smoked dope at university, he never inhaled. Others who took up smoking became hooked, having never been able to find anything else in their lives that could provide instant gratification on tap, several times a day; whereas Bill Clinton found Monica Lewinsky.

Having met your two-year target, you are now torn between your three options for disposing of the stockpile of tobacco:

selling up and enjoying the rewards of your abstinence; destroying it, so as to avoid feeling responsible for any ill-health that might be suffered by those who smoke it; and just giving it to smoker friends as an act of generosity.

You might feel that this last course of action absolves you of any moral guilt since you would not be profiting financially. But you need not be so hard on yourself. Whether you destroy this tobacco or donate or sell it to confirmed smokers will not affect them one way or the other: if they didn't get the tobacco from you, they would get it from somewhere else. Don't charge them if that makes you feel warmer but, ethically, it makes no difference.

Not my pigeon

Every day at 5.30 a.m., our neighbour throws food for pigeons on to her front lawn, near the boundary to our garden. As a result, pigeons congregate on our roof from about 5 a.m. in anticipation of their breakfast. This makes it noisy in the bedroom below, and the gutter is filled with pigeon waste. Should I ask my neighbour to stop putting food out for these pests?

Pigeons are beautiful and fly gracefully – No, wait! That's Nicole Kidman in the new movie version of *Bewitched* that I was thinking of. Pigeons? They are utterly unappealing. That's why God gave them that name, so that nobody could ever write a cute song about them, what with pigeon not rhyming with anything except smidgen and religion.

There's never an easy way to ease pigeon-related friction between neighbours. Shooting is an obvious option (the neighbours, not the pigeons), but may seem drastic. Mentioning this to your neighbour may persuade her to stop putting food out. But anyone who wakes so early to lay on breakfast for pigeons doesn't sound as if she'll be easily deterred.

What about erecting an effigy of Ken Livingstone? Pigeons smart enough to gather at 5 a.m. in readiness for a 5.30 a.m. feast may also be smart enough to know that London's mayor is their sworn enemy. Or put a cat among the pigeons. A big cat. Maybe tiger-sized. Or a model tiger, with tiger dung from a zoo, while you emit roars from your bedroom window. How much dung? A lot, not a smidgen; unless taunting a pigeon, is against your religion (see?).

Prophet motive

> *My son, thirteen, wants to earn some money from the craze for charity bracelets with a good-cause message. They sell in shops for £1 each, which goes to charity, but change hands at school for £3. If he buys £10 worth (charity gains) and sells for £30, can he keep all or some of the profit? Is it ethically OK to buy and sell not-for-charity copies?*

To achieve the greatest good, for the greatest number, your son should continue buying his fashionable bracelets from charity shops. He has then paid them the price they were asking for their bracelets, and owes them nothing further.

For him to buy and sell not-for-charity bracelets instead – on the ground that such bootleg bracelets would be part of a purely commercial, and thus guilt-free, chain of transactions between him and his school friends – might superficially seem ethically more clear-cut. But it would not benefit any charities at all and that would not be a satisfactory outcome.

The charities have reaped the reward they fully deserve for devising a fund-raising idea that milks the playground fascination for amassing collections; whether they be collections of football cards, of marbles, of charity bracelets, or of tall stories about sexual conquests. Though they probably wouldn't turn your son away if he chose to make an additional donation, the charities from which he bought the bracelets should have no ground for feeling cheated or duped if he re-sells them for profit; just as when we buy an object at a car-boot sale that we later sell for a profit, we are not duty-bound to track down the seller and give him a cut of our good fortune.

You can applaud your son's initiative. It's a useful lesson for any thirteen-year-old to learn that there are people rich enough, or lazy enough, to pay several times what a thing is actually worth. Most conceptual art, for instance.

Fat chance!

In a DIY superstore I noticed a grossly overweight lady with her equally overweight child aged about eight. When the child moaned she was bored, the mother handed her a bag of crisps and a chocolate bar. In my eyes, placating an already overweight child with inappropriate snacks is child abuse. Should I have intervened, or called the police or social services?

I just want to say that if you do get around to calling the police on this one, could you please let us listen in to the conversation? I mean, have you tried getting the police to come round to investigate a stolen car if they calculate that there's no chance that they'll be able to catch the culprits? ('Hello, police? Please, God, I've been able to reach you in time. I'd like to report an overweight mother giving her bored fat child inappropriate snacks in a DIY superstore. Hello? Hello? Is anyone there . . . ?') Most people would be very envious of your role in this matter, because you have so few other things to worry about that you are able to patrol DIY superstores as a suburban Superman, seeking out ugly behaviour so as to put society to rights.

There are many wrongs in the world; some big, some small; some that are our concern, some that aren't. We all make a mental grid of which wrongs we feel merit our interference. If someone isn't actually committing a crime, it's hard to persuade anyone – let alone a police officer – that this person needs apprehending. Why not arrest people for smoking, too? Or for sunbathing without adequate sun cream? You might be right to be concerned, but not to interfere.

8 Living: One Day At A Time

'I long ago came to the conclusion that all life is six to five against'

Damon Runyon

I take your point

> **?** *When the shopper in front of me at a store till was asked whether she had a loyalty card, she said that, unfortunately, she didn't. I joked that she could borrow mine. When she came to pay, she offered to load the points she'd have earned on to my card. Would it have been ethical to accept?*

It would have been unethical to accept in that a loyalty card is a store's inducement to shoppers to sign up to its bonus scheme for regular customers and, thereby, drum up repeat business ('bonus scheme for regular customers' being technical retailing jargon for 'giving customers a £10 voucher, which they can use only for buying even more goods from us, providing they first spend a sum in our stores equivalent to Cher's annual cosmetic surgery bills').

Loyalty points should be no more transferable to a fellow shopper than a London Underground one-day travel card is transferable to another would-be Tube passenger once you happen to have completed all your planned journeys for the day: yes, in theory, you could have made all those additional Tube journeys yourself. But the travel discount is an inducement for the specific purchaser of the travel card, as a ploy to swell overall ticket sales.

On the other hand, you might well think that it is the moral duty of each of us to confuse the nosey statisticians who exploit details of our shopping preferences stored in loyalty cards to glean useful information about us very cheaply. Your loyalty cards now contain enough information about what you've been buying and doing to blackmail you. If you really must have a loyalty card, swap it with others in the till queue so that the shop's statisticians are foxed by customers who seem to have no logical pattern of purchases from one week to the next.

oh, knickers!

I bought two packs of underpants from a leading high street chain. On trying on a pair this morning, I found that they came up to my armpits and were several sizes too big. The pants were worn only for a few seconds and I had just showered, so my dilemma is whether to return them and seek a refund, or just suffer the loss and be more careful when shopping in future.

Have you considered that, rather than a fresh pair of underpants, what you might need is a new pair of higher-prescription spectacles? Did you not notice, before slipping them on, that the pants seemed big enough not just to fulfil their intended purpose, but also to accommodate enough camping gear for a week's trekking in Snowdonia, while doubling up as a tent at night?

It's usually women who buy underwear in ambitiously generous sizes. Those push-up bras seem specifically designed to host breasts three sizes smaller than stated on the label.

Their trick is to turn each breast into a human iceberg – only one-ninth of which is visible to the eye, while suggesting a further (albeit phantom, as it turns out) eight-ninths of flesh hidden below eye-level.

Men, by contrast, underestimate their clothing size. A man will keep buying the same size of trousers/shoes/underpants even if he has metamorphosed over the years from being as thin as a whip to becoming too big to fit inside a telephone kiosk with the door closed. Only when he can no longer pull up his underpants even after strenuously levering himself into them with a shoehorn will he acknowledge that there is a problem. And the problem he will acknowledge is that his wife has carelessly shrunk his underwear in the wash.

Would you want to wear underwear worn by a stranger? Probably not. But all is not lost. Have you considered a camping trip in Snowdonia?

Giving them hell

I am a Christian. Though I am not a fundamentalist, I sincerely believe that anyone who fails to repent and trust in Jesus Christ will go to Hell. Is it ethical to respect the personal beliefs of others and basically let them go to Hell? Or should I warn them and risk upsetting them, not to mention the trouble I might cause for myself?

In a live-and-let-live age, many would say that it's no more your business to stop people from going to Hell, if that's what they want to do, than it is to stop them going to Wyoming, or to a cinema to watch *The Sound of Music* for the 197th time or to visit a plastic surgeon clutching a photo of Ernest Borgnine and pleading, 'Doc, I want you to make me look like *THIS!*'; just as it's nobody else's business to bully you with their belief that there is no Hell.

In any case, perhaps you should be sceptical of people who swear that they are atheists and don't believe in an afterlife. They may secretly be the most fervent believers of all: it may just be that they like to drive a hard bargain, and that they're trying to see how much extra they can squeeze out of God in return for finally being won around to his whole Hell concept. Moreover, civility demands that we indulge other people's religious beliefs every bit as tolerantly as we indulge their belief that they know how to crack the Middle East crisis, or that their hair actually looks good combed *that* way.

Anyway, some people actively want to go to Hell. Machiavelli reckoned that the company would be much better there – 'popes, kings, and princes, while in Heaven there are only beggars, monks, hermits and apostles'. And you have to admit this: when you watch people going to Hell, it often looks like they're having a pretty good time making their way there, doesn't it?

complete work of fiction

As an aspiring short story writer, I collect women's magazines that contain fiction. I sometimes see these in neighbours' recycling bins. Is it wrong to take these magazines without asking whether they're being thrown out anyway?

Listen, not only is it ethically OK to help yourself to these women's magazines in your neighbours' recycling bins, but you may even merit the *Al Gore Award for Outstanding Achievement in Recycling*, because by trawling through recycled magazines for guidance on how to compose the sort of short stories you read in women's magazines (which are themselves often crafted from prose that reads as if it was manufactured from recycled storylines culled from previous editions of women's magazines), you become the human pivot of a double-recycling enterprise that may well represent the ecological version of perpetual motion.

Study the facts: you collect recycled women's magazines to glean tips on how to write short stories for women's magazines; magazines that are later tossed into recycling bins, from which they are retrieved and recycled to provide tips on how to write short stories for yet more women's magazines. And so the virtuous circle continues: short stories helping to generate yet more women's magazines; and more women's magazines generating more short stories. It's the literary equivalent of a serpent swallowing its own tail (or, in this case, tale).

Here's the tricky part: short stories can lead to novels, just as petting leads to sex. Recycling magazines is one thing; pulping books, though, is bad form. The world's libraries are already teeming with unread books – like literary landfill sites. Do you promise to stick to short stories and avoid becoming an eco-menace?

These are the naked facts, lady!

> **?** *I exercise at an upmarket gym. After using a machine beside the office, I glimpsed a poster of a naked woman, plus a couple more of her in different poses. As a woman I feel uncomfortable, because the men who work there are probably viewing women in general as objects of sex. Surely this kind of thing is OK for private consumption, but not in a workplace?*

I really didn't want to be the one to break this to you, but a considerable number of quite normal men out there 'are probably viewing women in general as objects of sex' (I'm not talking about the ones using binoculars, obviously). It's how the world works much of the time. Or, at any rate, it's how Hollywood, the fashion industry, glossy magazine covers, the cosmetics business, *Sports Illustrated*'s annual *Swimsuit Issue*, and Bill Clinton work. Ask women if they view, say, John Prescott and Michael Moore as objects of sex, and many of them may grow queasy. Ask them the same about George Clooney and they're not quite so offended. Many might be even less offended by the possibility of George Clooney viewing them as a sex object.

All this doesn't mean that we should let our most basic instincts and desires dictate how we behave in public; otherwise people would all be trying to stick Angelina Jolie to a shop window using her lips as a suction pad.

Posters of nudes are not illegal, but it is insensitive to display them in a workplace, particularly in positions where customers of that workplace can glimpse them (much the way that Peter Stringfellow's hairdo is not illegal, yet it is insensitive to display it in a public place). It demeans women. Does that answer your question, love?

Said in camera

? *When I was buying a camera, the salesman demonstrated my chosen model and totted up the extras, which included an extended warranty. We had to have this, he said, because just before it expired we could stomp on the camera and claim another: manufacturers know that customers do this and factor it into the price. Should we have reported him to the manager? Or the manufacturer?*

To his credit, your camera salesman at least seems to have spotted the awkward paradox of spending half an hour making a pitch about a product's durability and reliability, before then persuading you that you really need to take out the extended warranty on the product because when it inevitably breaks down ('That's modern technology for you, sir'), the parts and labour for uninsured repairs could easily set you back more than your monthly mortgage repayments.

But with the security of an extended warranty contract you will have peace of mind. Should your camera/toaster/iron malfunction, you will be able to phone the manufacturer's extended warranty contract hotline number, where a helpful voice will immediately put you on hold on a premium-rate number until such time as the manufacturer thinks that it has recouped, via its phone revenue, any costs it is likely to incur in having to replace your goods. Salesmen push the extended warranty even when you're buying a £2.99 torch and the three-year extended warranty costs £4.99. They just can't help themselves. If they're at home, and their wife asks for a coffee, they ask whether she wants milk and an extended warranty with it.

Extended warranties are generally underwritten by insurers. The ethical course is to take your custom elsewhere and never to buy the extended warranty.

Lifted from the common crowd

While I was sharing a lift with three eight-year-old strangers yesterday, one of them spat on the floor next to me. I told him I thought that was a disgusting thing to do, and as I exited the lift he squirted my clothes with some horrible gunge. Was I right to say something?

You were certainly right to say something. It is a sad fact that when confronted by provocative anti-social behaviour from strangers, many of us – instead of boldly tackling them about their boorishness, as we have every right to do – respond by staring intently at our shoes as if we might be practising some kind of footwear hypnosis, saying nothing, breathing very quietly so as not to create any distraction whatsoever and hoping that the elevator doors open again before the yobs pummel us to a pulp. That's certainly MY response.

So the rest of us are relying on you to take a stand, and hope only that your pockets are deep enough to afford the dry-cleaning bills such stands are evidently likely to entail.

It's war, but on a smaller scale. We don't like to think of ourselves as appeasers. But if we lack the stomach for a fight, do we have any right to whine when the barbarians take over the castle? We tackle our pusillanimity in two key ways. First, by electing politicians to do the fighting for us (when John Reid became Britain's Home Secretary, many were hoping he would actually patrol lawless streets, meting out justice to thugs *in person*). The second way is by periodically venting our frustration on call-centre workers in India and Jakarta, because (a) we know that these people are too far away to come and hit us, and (b) they seem to have such a scant grasp of our bank affairs that we guess they won't know how to siphon funds out of our account by way of revenge.

commercial traveller

I enjoy watching many programmes on commercial TV. So am I morally obliged to watch the advertisements from companies that help to pay for these programmes? Or is it OK to change channels while the ads are on, or to fast-forward them when they are on videotape?

It's curious that the only TV channels without commercials are the shopping channels, whose entire schedule involves selling you things; usually things that you not only can't imagine anyone ever wanting to own or use but which you can't imagine anyone even thinking were worth spending their brief stay on this planet inventing.

Commercials are not part of some unspoken contract you enter into when watching commercial TV. It's not like having to listen to a lecture from the Salvation Army in return for getting a bowl of soup. The idea is that the programmes surrounding the ads should be so riveting that you'll want to watch that channel, and you will thus soak up the commercials shown during the breaks. The theory has suffered a little because (a) even lazy viewers now own remote controls, which means that switching channels, even briefly, no longer involves two trips from their sofa; (b) because there are only so many times you can watch some grinning celebrity telling you how to consolidate all your loans into one easy monthly payment without deciding that watching your children's DVDs of *Postman Pat* would be preferable; and (c) because TV stations often forget the part about making the programmes surrounding the ads riveting.

So advertisers now try to keep you hooked by making their ads entertaining. One day they may become so entertaining that viewers will surf channels between the commercial breaks.

Ball bearings

A golfing pal received from his son a present of golf balls imprinted with the sentence 'If found please return to Peter Smith'. This amused me, because it reflected the wayward nature of my friend's golf game. Last week I found one of these balls in the rough. Normally I would keep any ball found in the rough, but this time I can identify the owner. Should I return it?

Golfers are notoriously fretful about losing any of their very expensive golfing paraphernalia. This is why golfwear is manufactured in colours so luminous that you could spot a lost golfing sweater even from the window of a plane flying 30,000 feet above a golf course.

The downside of making misplaced golf clothes so easy to relocate is that the person who finds them may not be their rightful owner. So, cunningly, manufacturers protect such garments from being stolen by imprinting them with interlocking-diamond patterns, which deter anyone who finds a golf sweater from keeping it, lest his friends spot it in his wardrobe and wonder whether he's moonlighting as an Andy Williams impersonator. It takes a long time for a non-player to realise that when golfers talk about their handicap, they're not referring to their dress sense.

Can you identify the owner of a lost golf ball? Then you should return it. If you cannot divine the owner, Interpol won't lose sleep if you keep it. Only a cad calculates that, by not returning a lost ball, he's encouraging its owner to sharpen his game. Only an even bigger cad – on finding a named ball, and realising that he cannot keep it – would toss it still farther from the fairway, so that his friend's wayward tee-shot becomes the target of yet greater clubhouse mockery when the ball is eventually found; possibly by someone walking their dog in the next village.

Preserved fruit

When I was a child, and I accompanied my mother on supermarket shopping trips, before buying grapes she would always pick one to sample, often handing me a grape to taste, as well. As an adult I have thought nothing of trying a grape before buying the bunch. But now I wonder whether this is stealing. After all, I don't take a bite from an apple before I buy one.

There is little tradition of sampling before buying in Britain. For a country dubbed a nation of shopkeepers this parsimony has always seemed, at best, mean-spirited and, at worst, commercially short-sighted. At a street market in France or Italy, passers-by are encouraged to sample produce: vendors are confident that shoppers will be seduced by one mouthful. In American food malls it's hard to avoid all the hawkers urging you to sample their cookies, some pizza, a smoothie, some watermelon: if you were ruthless about it, and you didn't mind your entire diet being ingested in a pot-luck carnival of canapé-sized portions, you'd never need to pay for a meal again.

In my local street market I've seen mild-mannered stallholders screeching at Italians who help themselves to a grape before buying. They're as furious as if the tourist had just slain their first-born right there on the stall and was dripping the blood all over the apricots display. Supermarkets presumably factor in to their prices that people try grapes and cherries, just as some shoppers squeeze every avocado before choosing theirs. You even see people in supermarkets eating goods they haven't yet paid for, handing over an empty crisp packet for scanning at the checkout.

In a civilised world, you should be able to sample a grape – just as you might run your hands along a bolt of cloth, or take a Maserati for a test drive – before buying. If we are going to have Mediterranean weather in Britain soon, why not Mediterranean hospitality, too?

Driven to Lying

A local councillor who spent the general election campaign extolling the virtues of honesty and branding the Prime Minister a liar was caught speeding. She persuaded her daughter to say that she was driving. Shouldn't she be exposed as a hypocrite?

Someone should tell your errant councillor about a bargain that Adlai Stevenson offered to his political opponents during the 1952 American presidential election campaign. He promised that if they stopped 'telling falsehoods about us, I will stop telling the truth about them'. A politician calling another politician a liar is always a shamelessly entertaining spectacle. It's like William Hague calling Iain Duncan Smith 'baldy'; or Neil Kinnock accusing someone of being 'verbose, prolix, repetitive, long-winded and mighty wordy to boot, as well'.

Here is one of life's cuter paradoxes: many men and women stand for public office because they believe they can make their country a better place. These same men and women often also believe they have such an overwhelming duty to fulfil this calling that they may use whatever means are necessary to achieve electoral success, however indecent or underhand: these may include lying about a rival, or bugging the Watergate building to spy on your Democrat opponents.

Yes, your councillor is a hypocrite. One rider, though: should she not be judged by the same yardstick as those she represents? The ruse she used to avoid a driving ban has apparently become so commonplace now that even those with clean licences are accumulating penalties. On the other hand, it can't have been her first such offence. She may argue that she has only been speeding, the better to execute her public duties. The point is: can you believe her?

A pinch of herbs

While walking my child from school, I noticed a lush rosemary bush spreading from a garden on to the pavement. As I nabbed three sprigs to use in my dinner, the owner of the garden began knocking furiously on her window. The next day I bumped into the rosemary-bush owner, who scolded me for my 'appalling behaviour'. It was just a bit of rosemary. Did I behave so badly?

Logic tells you that a rosemary bush so flourishing that Helmut Kohl could hide in it and not be spotted will not miss a few sprigs being snipped from it. But logic, as Churchill pointed out, is a poor guide compared with custom. And do you know what the custom is in this instance? It's that you don't help yourself to samples from a stranger's rosemary bush without asking; just as you don't harvest a few of their holly branches at Christmas-time just to save you having to barter with the lone-toothed man who materialises in your local market every December and tries to charge you £7 for a diseased, two-foot-long stem of holly he probably just cut from a tree in the local park.

Anyway, logic can be a dull companion through life. Logic tells you it is unlikely that Nicole Kidman or Brad Pitt is ever going to pester you for sex; so you may as well stop daydreaming about the possibility of your having to fight off their advances, before grudgingly backing down and agreeing to move in with them (providing they promise not to become jealous if they see you talking to an attractive stranger). Who wants that kind of logic weighing them down?

Taking that rosemary didn't make the world shiver. Nobody died. Still, you should have asked, in the same way as you should ask before raiding a neighbouring table's bread basket in a restaurant. Or, at least, steal more discreetly.

Token effort

I received a correctly addressed communication from a mail-order firm, in which I found a letter addressed to a stranger, offering her a £5 voucher. Do I (a) put the whole thing in the bin and forget about it; (b) use the £5 voucher; or (c) relay the communication to the woman in question? My inclination is to do (a). My husband (a lawyer!) thinks that I should do (c).

Much as it may pain us to agree with a lawyer – if only for fear that he might take our nod of agreement as some kind of solicitation of his professional judgement, for which he will later bill us at £250 an hour (if you tried to tally lawyers' billing hours with their age, many lawyers would have to be at least 146 years old) – I think that your husband is right on this.

Of course, it's irritating to get mail tumbling through your letterbox that is meant for someone else, although given the way in which postal deliveries function nowadays, we have all got used to this: on many mornings your hall is like a mini-sorting office as you busily readdress envelopes to redirect misposted mail to its intended recipients. Maybe it's a trick that postal workers deploy for generating overtime work; you know, delivering the same letter two or three times over until it becomes as well travelled as Marco Polo.

But (and this is assuming that the £5 voucher is actually worth something, and not linked by an asterisk to small print explaining that it is redeemable only against orders totalling more than £400, and which also are placed in Manx dialect) you should do with the letter what you would wish a stranger to do with it had it been meant for you, but had popped through their letterbox. So (a) is not an option, and (b) is shabby, leaving (c). And I'm telling you that without charge.

Trial ride

On a bus to court for jury service, what I overhear a man say on his mobile phone leaves me in no doubt that he is guilty of a violent attack on another man. I later recognise him as the defendant in the case I am hearing. I should retire from the jury. But would it be unethical for me to stay silent about what I'd heard on the bus, and try to persuade my fellow jurors of his guilt?

Justice is like a debating society. The jury must decide whether a defendant is innocent or guilty based purely on the evidence they hear in the courtroom, not based on their hunches, prejudices or their determination to see someone get it in the neck, just because they happen to be having a bad day and want to make someone pay. What may seem curious, of course, is that the big decision on a defendant's guilt or innocence is made not by the one person in the courtroom who has enough in-depth knowledge of the law to make a reasonable stab at a well-weighted judgement – namely, the judge – but is made by twelve people who, very often, you wouldn't trust even to order for you in a restaurant. But that isn't proof that the jury system is a crock of poop. It may not be perfect, but it's still better than most of the other options.

How could you be sure that the defendant you overheard on the bus wasn't just recounting a quail-hunting trip with Dick Cheney? You are not Caesar, casting judgement with a swivel of your thumb. You are a juror who must draw a conclusion from only those facts presented to you inside a courtroom.

Justice must be transparent. It must not only be done, it must be seen to be done; even if sometimes, as J.B. Morton remarked, it must be seen to be believed.

Time is more than ripe

A tin of soup I bought at our small corner shop (the nearest supermarket is a twenty-minute walk away) turned out to be eight months past its sell-by date. And my husband bought a pack of sausages two weeks past their sell-by date. Do I report the shop, and deprive my neighbourhood of its nearest food supply, or let this potential source of food poisoning continue unchecked?

You are unwittingly contributing to – exacerbating, even – the problem that so vexes you. By avoiding buying groceries in your local corner shop because so much of its stock is past its sell-by date you are merely ensuring that even less of its stock is sold, and thus replenished with fresher items; which means that the next time you stop by, the goods on the shelves will be even further past their sell-by date, making you still more reluctant to shop there; and so on, until you'll walk in one day to find a tin of soup that has been waiting for a purchaser since roughly the Thatcher administration.

Equally, the more you shop at your local store, the greater its turnover will be, and thus the less chance there will be that the goods it stocks will have developed colonies of bacteria so ornate that only scientists will be keen on buying them for research purposes. So to some degree, matters are in your hands. Then again, it shouldn't be your burden to shop in a way that ensures that the produce in your local store is fit for human consumption.

But how to convey your unease discreetly? Invite the shopkeeper to dinner and tell him you'll be serving him his tinned soup and sausages.

Margin of error

A biography of Tolkien that I borrowed from a library referred to 'the American wit and author, Dorothy Sayers' – surely a reference either to the American wit, Dorothy Parker, or to the English author, Dorothy Sayers. I guess it is Miss Sayers, but don't know for certain. Is it better to write in the margin alerting future readers to the slip, or refrain from defacing a library book?

I don't know for certain, either, but I'd have plumped for 'American wit and author' fitting Dorothy Parker pretty well. So which is worse: having the biographer introduce an error (which many readers will spot as an error, even if they don't know whether he meant Sayers or Parker)? Or having you or me 'correct' the slip, in the process possibly introducing an even more vexing error, in as much as future readers will assume we must have been absolutely certain which Dorothy the biographer meant, or we wouldn't have annotated the margin?

Where would it stop? Would a reader be entitled to put a line through every page of *The Protocols of the Elders of Zion*, since the entire text is factually preposterous?

What about when a philosopher, economist or scientist puts forward a thesis that is coherent to them, but with which you quibble? Would you be entitled to scrawl through each page and scribble your own counter-argument in the margin? What about when an author has himself suggested that ideas he minted in a book when younger were not as rigorous as he once believed: the philosopher Freddie Ayer with logical positivism, for instance?

Does one have the author's tacit blessing to write 'Rubbish' across every page? What about fiction? May we also append our critical verdicts? Would there be a Barbara Cartland book left in a library undefaced?

Out of the frame

> *After a housemate, who was also a close friend, moved out about a year ago, I discovered that she had left her expensive camera. Despite my repeated reminders to her to collect it, she has never done so. Six months ago she stopped returning my calls, e-mails and texts. I assume that she has moved on in her life. I would like to know if I can consider the camera mine.*

Well, of course you can consider the camera yours; the same way you can consider Cate Blanchett your girlfriend. But does Cate Blanchett consider herself to be your girlfriend? What if the roles had been reversed, and you had left the camera behind: would you reckon it OK for your former housemate to now consider the camera hers? Your reply should give you a pretty accurate answer to your query. Oh, so you replied 'yes'? In that case we must persevere.

Unless you run a dry cleaning shop, or a shoe repair service, where you display a sign to the effect that 'all uncollected items will be disposed of by the management after three months', then you have no natural right ever to assume ownership of the camera. You have given your former housemate several opportunities to say: 'Oh, that old thing? You keep it!' She hasn't.

Then why doesn't she seem to be making much effort to retrieve her camera? Just life, I would guess. I could cite several objects dotted around my house that I vowed to move/return/bin/cook/sterilise/bury as much as a year ago;

especially bury. And sterilise. Yet all remain where I last left them – not unwanted; just undisturbed. A year is no time at all to ignore something that you might one day again find useful. Politicians do it with their consciences all the time.

child benefit

Although I am fifteen years old, I was recently refused entry to a film with a 15 certificate as I had no ID on me. Was I therefore justified in insisting on a child's ticket to see a PG film?

Y ou were refused entry to a film with a 15 certificate because the ticket-seller was seeking to uphold a law which seeks to prevent those under fifteen from being exposed to films they might find disturbing (although there doesn't seem to be any law protecting children from being exposed to films starring Keanu Reeves, which you'd have thought could scar a child for life).

The box office was not acting like a train ticket-seller, who might seek to establish a passenger's age in order to ensure that they are not trying to bilk the rail company by buying a child's fare when they are an adult. So to say that the box office's refusal to sell you a ticket to see a 15-certificate movie therefore entitles you to pay a child's tariff to see a PG film is missing the point, and counts as deception (or theft, if you want a blunter word).

The ticket-seller was trying to uphold the law, whereas you, by trying to buy a child's ticket to which you are not entitled, would be breaking the law. The cinema didn't say you weren't fifteen, merely that they had no evidence that you were fifteen. Were you to turn up at Heathrow without your passport,

passport control might say that they had no proof that you were a British citizen. But that wouldn't prove you aren't one: you couldn't turn their remark into an excuse to, let's say, avoid paying UK taxes, just because an immigration officer queried your citizenship.

Your argument has the allure of cute logic, but it is the verbal equivalent of an optical illusion.

Mass competition

? *I am an avid 'comper', and enter all the competitions that I can find. However, I am continually advised by other compers to enter every competition multiple times, in false names, because this increases my chances of success. Is this ethical?*

It may be ethically OK, but it might not be mathematically very astute. The world is divided into those who have the passion to enter every competition (on every crisp packet, on the back of every cereal box, convinced that they will one day win a year's supply of instant soup mix, or maybe a DVD boxed set of Linda Barker's TV commercials, which will transform their lives and bring untold joy) and the rest of us; who have lives.

What this means is that you are not competing for first prize against a random cross-section of the population. You are competing mostly against a hardcore of dogged compers, just like yourself. As each of these diehard compers enters every competition multiple times, the result is competition-entry inflation. So if each avid comper in the country – let's assume that there are 1,000 – enters a competition once each, each has an equal one-in-a-thousand chance of winning (so long as they can mint a snappy end to the tie-breaker sentence, 'I adore instant soup mix because . . .'). But if each comper enters the competition ten times, the total number of entries is 10,000; yet each comper still has only a one-in-a-thousand chance of victory. And if you're having to pay for your own postage for entries, you could even be nursing a net loss.

But hey, it's not all gloom: there's still an estimated nine-hundred-and-ninety-nine-in-a-thousand chance of *NEVER* winning a year's supply of instant soup mix or Linda Barker DVDs.

Tusk force

? *Being against the ivory trade, I want to dispose of an ivory necklace I was given years ago. If I sell it or give it to someone who doesn't object to ivory, I am perpetuating the view of ivory as a desirable item. Just burying it feels faintly ridiculous. What should I do?*

Burying the necklace sounds like an impotently symbolic gesture, assuming you're the only one who knows you have buried it. Of course, you could hold a little burial ceremony, but someone who has kept a necklace hidden away for years doesn't sound like a person who'd want to turn its disposal into an embarrassing song and dance (that's what we have Michael Flatley for).

Keeping it in a drawer does little but prick your conscience every time you lay eyes on it. Giving it away, or selling it? That might ensure that the necklace finds an appreciative home. But it might also prolong ivory's circulation in respectable society and lend it a sheen of fashionable desirability if the necklace is seen draped around the 'right' kind of throat.

People are easily influenced. For instance, when men see George Clooney wearing his hair fetchingly grey, they, too, may feel encouraged to ditch their hair dye and do likewise. Conversely, if people spot Ken Livingstone wearing a certain colour of shirt, they make a note never to buy clothes of that colour (even noticing that Livingstone has, say, eyebrows can be enough to make some people want to shave their own).

It is just this kind of repulsion, the sort triggered by negative role models, that offers a solution to your moral dilemma: sell your necklace to someone so dislikeable that, by wearing it, she becomes a roving ambassador for halting the ivory trade. Then donate the proceeds from your sale to elephant protection.

Gas ring

My upstairs neighbours claim that they have no gas meter in their flat. In that belief, they have paid no gas bills in seven years of living there, although they have gas central heating. My only comment has been to say how strange it is that there seems to be no meter. But it is both annoying and dishonest.

Once you've established that your neighbours are not getting a feed off your gas meter, resulting in your paying for their gas usage, what more do you propose doing, exactly? You could squeal to the gas supplier, although this probably won't make for great neighbourly relations. And even if you decided to phone your gas company, after twenty-seven minutes of being held in call-routing systems you might start stabbing your telephone keypad in frustration and anger ('Thank you. You pressed "Four", for "assault". If you know which household gas appliance you wish to shove down the operator's throat if you ever get to speak to a human being, please press "One" now').

Soon after that, you would realise that you'd rather scorch your own thighs with a blowtorch than wait on the phone even a second longer, at which point you might find that the whole idea of grassing up your neighbour palls. Not only palls, but you might even find yourself devising ways to enable all the flat-owners in your house to defraud this gas company, just to assuage your fury.

However, one matter that you and your upstairs neighbour have to clarify is whether they have a mains gas control switch (which is usually connected to the meter) that can isolate the gas supply in cases of emergency. Being spared seven years' worth of gas bills is not a sufficient return for the possibility of being blown up as a result of a gas leak.

Talking rubbish

> *Shortly after I stopped in a lay-by to eat a sandwich, a refuse collector arrived in his van to gather litter. Finishing my lunch, I dropped my sandwich wrapper in my car and drove on. But if everyone did as I did, the refuse collector might be out of a job. So would it have been more ethical for me to have dropped my wrapper in the next lay-by, instead of taking it home?*

The only tricky part about being blessed with your degree of moral probity is that there can't be enough hours in the day for you to execute all the good deeds you may wish to carry out. Along with strewing litter, there are also crimes to be committed, to ensure that police need never fear redundancy; and there's all that fatty food to eat, so that cardiologists may be sure of funding a plump pension on the proceeds of your custom. You probably feel guilty, too, if you don't regularly let the bath overflow, so as to provide work for decorators. Arson is an ugly word, used by those who give no thought to the livelihood of others: without people like you spending their weekends selflessly starting blazes, how could firemen rely on a steady income?

In short, littering is not an act of kindness towards rubbish-collectors. Collecting litter is a burden on taxpayers, who would far rather redirect the money spent on picking up your sandwich wrappers to equip hospital wards, or to fund theatres, or to buy library books.

When John Maynard Keynes suggested alleviating Britain's unemployment crisis by getting labourers to dig holes and fill them up again, this make-work scheme was designed to lift the country out of severe depression: it had an economic rationale, not a moral one.

In some respects

Should I respect a man who shows me none in return? If so, how is this defensible?

You might respect a man – a great statesman, say, or novelist, or philanthropist – who shows you none in return simply because he does not even know who you are. You might respect a man who is personally known to you, and you to him, who shows you no respect in return because, though this man may possess qualities worthy of your respect, he happens to be somehow flawed as a human being: such a combination is not uncommon with people who are geniuses in their field; albeit flawed geniuses. Great men, in many fields, are often forgiven for aberrant, rude, careless, inconsiderate behaviour by family and friends on the ground that their talents somehow excuse them from being judged as lesser mortals are judged. (This is in contrast to people who also behave in rude, careless, inconsiderate ways, but have no compensating talent; who are just classed as bullies; or possibly as Simon Cowell.) Respect is a tricky commodity all round. For instance, when people say 'with all due respect', they are often about to show very little respect: particularly if they are saying 'with all due respect' while standing in a courtroom, addressing an implausible defendant, and wearing a matted grey wig that makes it look as if an aged stoat has died on their head.

Respect is not a transaction: if you're lucky, you might reap some in return whenever you dispense some. But it is not like visiting a bureau de change and handing over dollars in exchange for an equivalent amount of euros. It is closer to admiration; or even love. Respect is given with no expectation of its being returned, although with much hope that it will.

Fishy practice

This morning the bin men made their weekly collection. This evening I had kippers for tea. A whole week to go, but the remains of the kippers that tasted so good now smell so bad. There's a public wastebin a few yards down the road. Problem solved?

If only scientists would devote a tenth of the effort to eliminating household cooking smells that they devote to improving dishwasher tablets, your problem would be solved. Every time you visit a supermarket you notice that there's been yet another breakthrough in dishwasher-tablet technology. Maybe you could wash your kipper carcasses in your dishwasher, leaving them so spotless that there's nothing left to create a stink.

When a woman recently complained to her council that its switch from weekly to fortnightly rubbish collections left her with a dilemma over what to do with her chicken bones (left in a bin indoors for a fortnight, they'd stink the house out; left outdoors for two weeks, they'd attract every fox and rat in the neighbourhood), her local environmental services officer told her it wasn't so smart of her to eat roast chicken just after the dustmen had visited ('Mummy! Why the roast chicken treat for dinner? Is it bin day tomorrow?'). Or, he suggested, why not freeze the chicken bones for a fortnight until the next garbage collection?

Loopy? Yes. But no more mischievous than exporting your domestic stink to the public. To punish passers-by with the smell without their having even enjoyed the treat would be as unethical as seizing a stranger off the street to wash your dishes. Assuming you didn't have a dishwasher, that is. And if you need advice on dishwasher tablets, I'm here.

Café culture

As I got my coffee in a café, a customer departed, leaving his newspaper on the table. The café asks customers to pay for their newspapers, displayed on a stand. A waitress returned the man's newspaper to the stand for resale. Am I justified in taking the paper from the stand to read it without paying?

More testing times in coffee bars, then. First there was the worry of whether you would ever manage to locate, on the bar menu listing eighty-seven different configurations of coffee, the one that equated to 'just coffee, with milk, served in a cup smaller than a tureen. No skinny anything, no wings. You know, just like in Italy' before you reached the head of the queue. And now this.

A café reselling a newspaper it has already sold to a previous customer is as cheeky a practice as using the dregs in a customer's wine glass to top up the house claret. But just because the café has no right to charge twice for the same newspaper, does it mean that you may read it without paying, on the ground that it has already been paid for by a previous patron?

On returning to your hotel late at night, you often see room-service dinner trays outside guests' doors, awaiting collection. Often the trays contain uneaten food. It would be unethical for a hotel to recycle this food. But does that mean it is ethical for you to help yourself to a bread roll and a snick of smoked salmon on the ground that since the hotel can't recycle the leftovers, and the diners have finished with them, who would you be hurting by digging in?

In both cases you are behaving unethically: you paid nothing for the newspaper, or for the hotel snack. The latter trespass is more forgivable. Or, at any rate, requires a less thick skin.

Trap-ease

? *After spotting a mouse in my kitchen, I bought a trap and caught it. The next night I caught another, smaller one, presumably its mate. Since then there has been no sign of any others in the house. Should I continue to bait the mousetrap with chocolate and cheese to entice more mice in from outside, or wait until I see them intruding into my space before catching them?*

You have a right to rid your kitchen of unsanitary vermin. It may not be their fault that mice are generally weaker than humans, thus giving mouse-hating humans the upper hand in any turf war, but that's the way of the world. Yes, it may be true that all life is sacred, but it is also true that some life is more sacred than others. Even those who wouldn't hurt a flea might wonder how they would react if their baby was about to be savaged by a bear or a rabid pit-bull – and they happened to have a shotgun to hand.

But your right to dispatch a trespassing mouse doesn't mean that you also have the right to see off anything that is weaker than you, smaller than you, and can't afford a fancy lawyer to plead its cause. If that were the case, the world would be ruled by Mike Tyson's thighs.

Your goal was to rid your house of intruders. Having satisfied yourself that you have seen off the mice that were using your place as a free bed and breakfast, continuing to lay out bait might be regarded as a form of entrapment. If mice are no longer bothering you, then you no longer have any right to bother them – just as a sheep farmer might be within his rights to shoot a dog that is off the leash in his sheep meadow, but would be breaking the law if he wandered around the village shooting any Labradors he suspected might one day menace his livestock.

Paper currency

? *The station from which I commute is provided with newspapers by a local newsagent, with payments put into an honesty box. Sometimes lacking exact change, I overpay one day, underpay the next. But some don't pay at all, and the newsagent is threatening to end the arrangement. Am I, too, technically stealing? Should I buy a paper only when I have exact change?*

It is always heart-warming to hear of an adult human being still relying on the kindness of strangers. It is especially heart-warming when those strangers are rail commuters, a species whose own faith in humanity has been shredded by a lifetime of implausible platform announcements about train delays.

One option would be to pay a cheque at the newsagent's shop at the start of each week to cover your bill in advance: your conscience would be clear and the newsagent's books would be balanced. But would that secure the future of your newsstand? How would a fellow commuter be able to distinguish between you and one of those people taking a paper and not paying at all?

This problem would also arise if you overpaid one day and drew on your credit the next. If a commuter is shameless enough to steal a newspaper, he is also shameless enough to give the impression that he, too, has paid in advance for the paper that he is taking. Very soon most honest commuters will feel tyrannised by the dishonesty of a few of their fellow passengers. When it comes to an honesty box, payments must not only be made, they must be seen to be made.

Not cricket

? *My family and I were at a cricket match. A man sat behind us with his young son who constantly made disgusting sniffing noises, clearly in need of a tissue. I was tempted to complain, but didn't want to make a scene or have to move seats. What should I have done?*

A major purpose of children is as a test: to test your patience; to test if you're greedy enough to eat the leftovers of your infant's pureed lunch; to test if you have the stamina to stick with parenthood, or whether your exciting new baby will end up in the loft after six weeks, gathering dust alongside the Rolf Harris *Stylophone*.

As a rule, you should be tolerant towards other people's children; unless their heads spin in circles and they continually invoke the Devil, like Linda Blair in *The Exorcist*.

Confined spaces are particularly testing. Parents on aircraft, for instance, are fully aware that flying for seven hours within earshot of a stranger's baby is as relaxing as sharing a party wall with someone learning to play the drums. As their infant wails like a siren, the mother winces apologetically at her fellow passengers while bribing the child with toys, food, drink and early access to its inheritance. The father sits nearby, not entirely distancing himself from the commotion, but not actively participating either, as if he might be a police officer escorting the mother and child back to their native country following extradition proceedings.

So no, don't complain. Smile sympathetically at the boy's father, mentioning how colds seem to be doing the rounds, and offering some tissues. Don't be deterred even if he acts like he's just a plain-clothes policeman accompanying the child on a day-release prison outing.

Tenants see agreement

Tenants who rent my flat have not paid rent, have caused damage to the property, assaulted neighbours, and generally been hell. Should I inform their referees, who provided glowing references as to their behaviour?

Human beings can be like multi-faceted prisms in the number of faces we expose to the world. A sports teacher who vouches that a pupil is an excellent sprinter is not in a position to confirm whether he is also a shoplifter if he has no proof of this. Similarly, a policeman telling the sports teacher that the boy is a shoplifter will not make him any less speedy a sprinter in the eyes of his sports teacher.

You have seen an ugly side of your tenants which may not necessarily have been witnessed by their referees. As a result, details you pass on to these referees about your tenants' misbehaviour might be as surprising to the referees as their testimonials now seem to you.

The whole business of references is a circular nonsense, anyway. Who asks for a reference from someone they know will furnish a bad one? When have you ever phoned a referee for a jobseeker, or a builder, or a nanny, and been told: 'What? They gave you my name as a referee? After what they did to us, and the court case, and the restraining order and everything?'

For a meaningful reference we should just ask prospective employees or tenants to provide an outline of their life and allow us to phone, at random, someone in their office, or a contemporary of theirs at university, and ask: 'Do you remember a guy called Tom Flimwell who was at university with you? Was he a big cheat in exams? Did he buy his round?

He was? He didn't? But, hey, what about you, you sound respectable? Need a job? Or a flat?'

Hero or zero?

My MP is hardworking, honest, and tries to do his very best for his constituents. On a personal basis I would not hesitate to vote for him. His party, however, stands for several principles that I find morally reprehensible, and its leader is untrustworthy. Do I vote for the man who does so much for me and my neighbours but whose party is morally bankrupt, or for a man with no track record in the constituency but whose party has aims with which I agree?

Your local MP is honest? Hard-working? Tries his very best for his constituents? And you're thinking of abandoning him? For most people, politics offers a choice between the awful and the unthinkable. You are lucky to face at least one option that you find palatable. The leader of the party to which your MP belongs may strike you as wholly untrustworthy, but no party is ever as bad as its leaders.

Your dilemma is how to weigh up the known good that your MP does for your community against the harm that you fear the leader of his party might inflict on the country as a whole. Are you being selfish in putting your neighbourhood's wellbeing first? No, you are not. Democracy is built from small building blocks. Together these rise to a peak, which is called the prime minister (although prime ministers are called other things once in office). If the foundation stones are solid, the structure should also prove secure. Democracy doesn't work the other way round. A premier cannot dictate how all his party's MPs should vote on every issue – unless all these MPs are spineless toadies who prize their own parliamentary ambitions above the needs and concerns of their constituents. Wait, this is where we came in, isn't it?

If you still yearn to be represented by someone who knows how best to rule Britain but doesn't actually get round to doing anything, why not vote in a local taxi driver?

Peek time

? *Walking to work last week, with the sun behind, I noticed that the outfit worn by the businesswoman in front of me had been rendered completely transparent by the light. Should I have told her, or would she have assumed that I had been looking rather too closely?*

That's why people say that any man who says he can see through a woman is missing a lot. It would have been wrong, following this serendipitous sighting, to have then altered your route to work in order to continue assessing the spectacle. But assuming you just gained a momentary frisson from a glimpse of the woman's body silhouetted against the sunshine, then you may treat it as a transitory wonder of nature: such as glimpsing a rainbow.

Assuming you weren't stalking the woman, there is no particular onus on you to inform her that she is wearing a see-through outfit, any more than it is your duty to tell a stranger in the street that he has an implausible hairdo (even if that stranger is Phil Spector). And remember, half the world's press snapped that famous photograph of an innocent Diana Spencer – her legs clearly visible against the sunshine through her flimsy skirt – without bothering to mention that the image would haunt her for years to come.

But you may still feel it honourable to inform the businesswoman, so that she might attend to the problem. So should you? Tell me, how good-looking are you? Do you look like Charles Laughton? Then chances are she may take you for a Peeping Tom. If, though, you resemble Daniel Craig in *Casino Royale*, she may well flush coquettishly. I know, I know, it's not logical. But no one said it was easy to see through women. Not in that sense, anyway.

utterly barking

? *I have a Labrador which is out of hand and has torn up my garden and eaten several of the ducklings from my pond, so I must let it go. It enjoys a good chase in the outdoors, so would it be ethical to pass it on to my local hunt and allow them to chase it about the countryside unto death?*

Of course it would. Just as it would be equally ethical to condemn your granny to the same fate if she should ever grow so incontinent and forgetful that she becomes a nuisance to have around. Same goes for any toddler who throws tantrums and won't eat up his broccoli.

Your Labrador isn't aware of the damage it's causing to your garden or to your flock of ducklings because it knows no better, on account of it having the mental faculties of a guava. But many creatures with modest brains succeed in living happy lives, full of contentment and quiet achievement. Some even become politicians, a life which – like that of a dog – also involves seeking out messes deposited by predecessors who travelled along that same path, poking one's nose into them, creating even bigger messes than those they found, and then scampering off in the hope that some other creature will inherit the blame for their handiwork.

It is not your dog that hasn't thought out the consequences of tearing up your garden and eating your ducklings, it is you who haven't thought out the consequences of owning a frisky Labrador. Should you now find yourself feeling so guilty about this oversight that you feel you deserve to be chastised, you could always inquire if your local hunt could chase you about the countryside unto death.

A real earful

? On returning home from buying an iPod, a colleague discovered that the retailer had given her not the 30GB model she'd requested and paid for, but an 80GB iPod, costing about £70 more. She has had sleepless nights of guilt about the shop assistant's error. Should she exchange it at the shop for the 30GB iPod, or just keep it – and with it the extra 12,500-song capacity?

An 80GB iPod stores about 20,000 songs. Listening to all those songs – assuming that each track lasts five minutes – would take seventy days, earphones plugged in day and night; or roughly the amount of time it takes for the cost estimate for the London Olympics to treble yet again.

Assuming that you lead any kind of normal life, that's several years' worth of iPod-listening right there. Is that what your colleague needs? Or is she the type who actually listens to only 500 or so tracks, but likes to keep a further 19,500 within reach, just in case she's struck by a sudden ache to hear the original cast recording of *Oklahoma!*? That's like taking your entire wardrobe on holiday because your airline has waived all baggage limits and (who knows?) you might fancy wearing a shirt you haven't worn since 1992; or an opportunity might finally arise to wear that lime-green designer dress that was reduced by £680 in a sale (and which was put there because sales staff had complained about it having given them all retinal damage).

Sleepless nights are your subconscious mind's way of telling you that you have done something you really shouldn't have and now regret; or else that you ate a hot dog you bought from a barrow-vendor near Trafalgar Square at 2 a.m. on a Saturday – no wait, I'm just repeating myself there. For both practical and ethical reasons, the 80GB iPod should go back to the shop.

No funny business!

> *Neighbours' cats defecate in our garden. We bought a dog to chase them away, but the cats still visit our garden at night. My neighbours seem to think it amusing. Would I be pushing the point too far if I resorted to tossing my dog's mess over the fence into my neighbour's garden?*

Neighbours, eh? You can't live with them, you can't shoot them without getting arrested. One problem with cats is that they don't scare easily. That's what comes of having nine lives: you feel you can afford to live a little dangerously. So intimidation is not an option. Anyway, cats behave pretty much as they please. They don't even bother getting dressed in the morning. They do what they want, when they want. That's why you never see a cat setting its alarm, or asking you for the time: they don't make appointments they have to keep.

Tossing your dog poop over fences isn't an option, either. Presumably you've tried all the products on the market that are supposed to keep cats away and found them wanting. Some people swear by lion dung as a cat deterrent, assuming you can find a co-operative lion. Kidnapping is too extreme, and doubtless illegal, although wasn't it intriguing to read that recent story of a cat called Emily that vanished from her home in the American Midwest and resurfaced three weeks later in eastern France? Apparently Emily had padded into a paper warehouse in Wisconsin, been accidentally boxed up amid bales of paper, and was shipped 4,200 miles to Nancy, France, where the employees of a paper factory unwrapped her. Does Emily's disappearance sound suspicious to you? And strangely appealing, too? It does? Then you need to be restrained before you embark on a course you will regret.

Taking it too easy

We are moving to a smaller house, so we put out a heap of bric-a-brac on the front garden with a notice saying 'help yourself'. Too late, I realised that some of the bottles had been used for storing garden and kitchen chemicals. What should I do?

Many people are seeking to trade down to a smaller house to cash in on the property boom, only to find that by the time they've flogged their big house, the price of the smaller house they coveted has swollen so much that it's now pricier than the bigger house they just sold.

Given how much they profit when house prices zoom, you'd think estate agents might try to find fresh ways to make house-buyers feel better about their having to sell a kidney to afford a roof to sleep under. But their pitch never varies: 'It's got a great view', they say, when the only view that would justify the asking price would be a view of Niagara Falls in moonlight. And to divert attention from a house so small that a mouse would find it cramped, the agent hawks it as 'a perfect opportunity to have a clear-out'. Is that how you landed yourself in this mess?

If you lend someone your car, knowing that the brakes are faulty, you bear some blame if he has an accident. But passers-by who pick up stuff left on the street largely assume responsibility if, say, they prick themselves on a protruding nail from a bookshelf. If they took clothes, for instance, they wouldn't assume you'd already had them dry-cleaned. Only a dork would use bottles picked up from the street to store baby-milk formula or mouthwash. Still, an advisory follow-up notice wouldn't hurt. But just whose life is so lacking in glassware that it is improved by salvaging hand-me-down bottles?

Stalling for a long time

? *Despite booking six months in advance for a popular London show, I could only get Friday matinee tickets for my family, so I'll have to take my daughter out of school early that day. The last time something similar arose, her school responded curtly to a request for time off. So I'm thinking of lying and just saying she has a dentist's appointment. Would that be wrong?*

If dentists got paid for all the phantom appointments they were supposed to be fulfilling, along with all the genuine ones they do fulfil, they'd be so rich they'd all have retired to Monaco by now and we'd have no dentists left. That would force people to invent new excuses for absences from their school or workplace: chiropody, maybe ('Please Miss, I have to leave school early today to see my chiropodist.' TEACHER:

'Whoah! Keep those scary teeth hidden when you're talking to me! Have you considered flying to Monaco for some urgent dental work?').

You might have thought that teachers and bosses would have started to suspect something by now: it's not as if all this dental work has done us much good. To an American, the only thing funnier than the sight of an English set of teeth is hearing that Arnold Schwarzenegger accidentally rubbed himself down with haemorrhoid cream instead of body oil and his breasts shrank to the size of pimples.

Schools know that the odd afternoon spent on some useful adventure can teach a child more than a week spent in a class-room. But schools also have to avoid a free-for-all. Dental appointments have become a code by which parents and schools communicate this understanding, without setting an awkward precedent. Both also know that white lies educate a child in how the adult world works – and we have the teeth to prove it.

Nose dive

At a dinner, a gentleman I was talking to took such a big sneeze into his handkerchief that I actually noticed part of his sneeze sailing into my food. I couldn't ask our hostess to serve the food again. Nor could I leave it. So I made some comment about 'turning away would have been nice', gritted my teeth and ate it. Was my neighbour in the wrong, or was I for minding?

If you've read those exposés of what goes on in restaurant kitchens away from the prying eyes of diners, then (a) you might never eat out again unless you had a table in the restaurant's kitchen from where you could watch the chefs prepare your meal before your eyes, and (b) you might have shrugged philosophically when your dinner-party neighbour sneezed into your supper and thought, 'Better the body fluid you know, than the body fluid you don't know'.

It is certainly disheartening to track the trajectory of someone's sneeze into your stew, but chances are your dinner would have been just as contaminated had the sneezer been sitting at the far end of the room. Sneezes, like stealth bombers, can travel astonishing distances, at physics-defying speeds, undetectable by radar or human eyesight: launching satellites is an expensive business, but if they ever invent a satellite small enough to fit inside a nostril, you could propel it into orbit just by tilting your head backwards and sneezing it into space.

We are surrounded by germs. Thankfully, most of them are invisible, or we would be so depressed about our unsanitary surroundings that we'd have no leeway to sink still deeper into gloom whenever we heard *Coldplay* on the radio. Also, studies show that a little dirt and a few germs strengthen your immune system (albeit not enough to withstand prolonged exposure to *Coldplay*).